# Structural Change and Competitive Dynamics in Global Financial Markets

Mehmed Ganić

# Structural Change and Competitive Dynamics in Global Financial Markets

## The Catalytic Role of Two Crises

palgrave
macmillan

Mehmed Ganić
International University of Sarajevo
Sarajevo, Bosnia and Herzegovina

ISBN 978-3-032-28905-6 ISBN 978-3-032-28906-3 (eBook)
https://doi.org/10.1007/978-3-032-28906-3



This Palgrave Macmillan imprint is published by the registered company Springer Nature Switzerland AG
The registered company address is: Gewerbestrasse 11, 6330 Cham, Switzerland

# Preface

Globalization has made Western economies and financial systems dominant worldwide. The financial sector has changed considerably due to the advent of new intermediaries and financial instruments and the growing globalization of financial markets. Nevertheless, the recent global financial crisis (GFC) has demonstrated the need to transform the global financial market along the Western-centric line. Several challenges developing regions encounter in this regard. These are deteriorating financial market imbalances, inflows of foreign direct investment (FDI), and increased exposure to financial volatility.

This book is a product of the current uncertainty that has been affecting the global financial markets over the past few decades. Those in charge of global capital flows continually face two closely related forces: the rapid transfer of financial power to Asia and the abrupt fluctuations in global capital flows.

These tendencies are not simple statistics; they represent profound changes in the world economy that significantly affect business, politics, and society. The emergence of Asian financial hubs, the maturation of international financial markets, and their growing impact on international transactions have become so important that they are being closely monitored. However, the driving force behind writing the book is growth rather than crisis. The global financial system is caught in an endless cycle of instability, and the impact of major players and institutions on it is becoming increasingly influential. The world's major financial centers, which are responsible for distributing international capital, are also contributing to systemic problems.

The GFC and the COVID-19 pandemic are events that cannot be forgotten. Instead of establishing new financial powers, they strengthened the trends. This crisis exposed structural vulnerabilities and resilience in the international financial markets, making them more competitive. The researchers are interested in finding answers to this crisis by studying how it can both increase prices and influence the Asian market by altering the global financial system, as well as what it implies for the future of financial centers, capital markets, and the world economy. We believe that this book will be of value to academia, financial market practitioners, and all individuals who want to understand the forces that have transformed the world financial system as we know it.

The book outlines four key insights for academic literature. First, it examines global financial developments since the onset of the COVID-19 pandemic. In fact, this study includes data through 2023–2024 and examines the pandemic transition strategy alongside the interest rate cycle, unlike the 2019 and 2020 studies. Second, it explores the "global financial cycle," highlighting regional variations, especially in Asia, where demand for Chinese corporate bonds grows independently of the US business cycle. Third, it offers systematic cross-regional quantification of market depth, efficiency, and resilience, demonstrating that the quality of financial integration differs more than its quantity. Fourth, it argues that these trends will influence the China-US relationship, especially regarding whether China seeks to replace the US, which affects how the emerging duopoly—accounting for 55.6% of total income—will coexist. This will be more complex than existing dominance or crowding-out models.

I wish to give my heartfelt thanks to Tula Weis, senior editor at Palgrave Macmillan New York, who played a critical part in the publishing of the book. Nevertheless, her professionalism is not only alive but also inspirational. I also wish to thank the anonymous reviewers whose positive remarks, knowledge, and ideas significantly enriched this book.

Sarajevo, Bosnia and Herzegovina, 11 June 2026 Mehmed Ganić

# Acknowledgments

*I owe my gratitude to my mother, wife, and two lovely daughters, who gave me moral support and kept me alive with endless patience and love throughout this process and in my life.*

# Abbreviations

| | |
|---|---|
| AUD | Australian dollar |
| BCBS | Basel Committee on Banking Supervision |
| BIA | Basic indicator approach |
| BIS | Bank for International Settlement |
| CAB | Current account balance |
| CAC | Cotation Assistée en Continu |
| CAD | Canadian dollar |
| CAGR | Compound annual growth rate |
| CAR | Capital adequacy ratio |
| CHF | The Swiss franc |
| CNH | Offshore Chinese yuan |
| CNY | Chinese yuan |
| CRD | Capital requirements directive |
| CRAR | Capital to Risk-Weighted Asset Ratio |
| CRR3 | Capital requirements regulation |
| CVA | Credit valuation adjustment risk |
| DAX | Deutscher Aktienindex |
| DCM | Debt capital market |
| EBA | European Banking Authority |
| EM | Emerging markets |
| ESG | Environmental, social, and governance |
| EU | European Union |
| EUR | Euro |
| FDI | Foreign Direct Investment |

| | |
|---|---|
| FED | Federal Reserve System |
| FIRB | Foundation internal ratings-based approach |
| FX | Foreign exchange |
| FSB | Financial Stability Board |
| FOREX | Foreign exchange |
| FPI | Foreign Portfolio Investment |
| FRTB | Fundamental Review of the Trading Book |
| FTSP | Financial Times Stock Exchange |
| GBP | Great Britany Pound |
| GDP | Gross domestic product |
| GDPPC | Gross domestic product per capita |
| GFCI | Global Financial Centers Index |
| GFC | Global Financial Crises |
| G-SIBs | Global systemically important banks |
| HKD | Hong Kong dollar |
| IFI | International Financial Integration |
| IFC | International Financial Center |
| IMF | Internal model |
| IMF | International Monetary Fund |
| IRB | Internal ratings-based |
| JPY | The Japanese yen |
| LCR | Liquidity coverage ratio |
| LR | Leverage ratio |
| MENA | Middle East and North Africa |
| MNC | Multinational corporation |
| NFA | Net foreign asset |
| NFC | Non-financial corporations |
| NSFR | Net Stable Funding Ratio |
| OFC | Other financial corporations |
| OTC | Over the counter |
| SA | Standardized approach |
| SDR | Special drawing rights |
| SGD | Singapore dollar |
| SMM | Standardized measurement method |
| STCAP | Stock market capitalization |
| TSA | Standardized/alternative standardized approach |
| TSX | Toronto Stock Exchange |
| U.S. | United States of America |
| USD | The United States dollar |
| UK | The United Kingdom |

# Contents

# List of Tables

# List of Figures

CHAPTER 1

# Introduction

**Abstract** When severe financial crises occur, they do not simply create new financial hierarchies. On the contrary, crises reinforce existing trends, expose structural weaknesses, and alter the existing level of global competition. This book demonstrates three key changes in the financial sphere. First, the US–China duopoly and the multipolar financial system; second, the growth of debt markets relative to banks; and third, the contrast between the strength of the Asia-Pacific region and the weakness of Europe.

**Keywords** Competitive dynamics in finance • financial globalization • Structural change in global finance • Regulatory convergence • and IFCs' resilience and adaptation

Financial globalization, which began with the collapse of the Bretton Woods system in 1973, has undergone several phases. These included the expansion of the Eurodollar market in the 1970s, the rapid liberalization in the 1980s, the market-wide crisis in the 1990s, and the rule changes after 2008. The conditions for structural change and contingencies were developed in each phase. Although not a new trend, the GFC marked the collapse of the Western-centric banking model that had existed since the 1980s (Lane, 2012). In recent decades, the expansion of corporate debt


M. Ganić, *Structural Change and Competitive Dynamics in Global Financial Markets*,
https://doi.org/10.1007/978-3-032-28906-3_1

and growth in emerging markets have been aided by low interest rates and quantitative easing, policy responses to the crisis. The consequences of the COVID-19 pandemic in 2020–2021 were largely the same. It did not bring about a new trend in digital finance, bank bailouts, or monetary stimulus; on the contrary, it set that trend in motion. It also caused divisions across regional markets, reinforced the technology sector's dominance (as evident in the US market), and contributed to the contrast between stagnation in Europe and resilience in Asia.

The book seeks to analyze this phenomenon, identify stable and unstable structures, and explore how the dynamics of global financial markets are evolving.

This book's main idea is that major financial crises, such as the 2008 global financial meltdown and the COVID-19 pandemic, do not establish new financial hierarchies. Instead, they speed up existing trends, expose structural flaws, provide both stability and flexibility, and continuously reshape competition in global finance.

It is possible to draw three conclusions from this book:

To begin with, the distribution of financial power in the Asia-Pacific region is a major contributor to the development of capitalism, trade, and financial integration and growth. This can be attributed to the US-EU-Japan financial triangle having shifted into a US-China duopoly. It is not separation but diversification: old centers retain their dominance, whereas new centers are open to movement and progress.

The other problem is that sustainability is relatively new, and it entails associated requirements. A critical evaluation across all chapters indicates that diversity and structure are less significant than depth. In contrast to markets that depend on a single instrument, the ability to access diverse sources of financing, e.g., sovereign debt, bonds, direct investors, and companies, makes them more resilient to adverse impacts. Following the GFC, the system relied on banks, and the COVID-19 pandemic increased demand and exacerbated geopolitical conflict for Ukraine. Third, competitive dynamics have fundamentally changed, where several common determinants, such as regulatory flexibility, technological advancement, geopolitical stability, and market depth, determine the attractiveness of capital flows. For example, IFCs that guarantee wealth, predictability, flexibility, and stability are likely to be useful in the next decade. This is why San Francisco is surging, Tokyo is falling, Paris is booming, and London is stagnating. It also discusses the reasons Singapore has consolidated its position despite Hong Kong's political instability.

This book explores this issue and builds upon the previous research in at least five ways to solve this problem:

The initial one is to expand the discussion of IFCs (Cassis & Wojcik, 2018). As demonstrated in this book, although past studies have indicated that financial institutions are unusually resilient in the face of crises, this study finds that resilience is merely a cover for structural issues. We conclude that IFCs have survived due to their regulatory flexibility, adaptability to technological change, and geopolitical positioning. That is why basic rankings will no longer reflect the entire diversity of rivalry in financial centers.

Second, it assesses the existing balance of power between the US and China, which generates a persistent debate over the world's power casters (Farrell & Newman, 2019; Starrs, 2019; Winecoff, 2020; Li, 2025). Although there is ongoing debate among researchers about China's interest in maintaining US dominance, data on fixed-income securities show that China and the US together hold 55.6% of the world's outstanding fixed-income securities (2023), up from 40.9% five years earlier. This trend signifies diversification rather than displacement: the historical centers of power remain influential, while emerging players gain strength.

Third, the book re-examines the relevance of the debate initiated by Lane and Milesi-Ferretti (2001) on financial integration. Several recent studies, building on Lane and Milesi-Ferretti (2001), have re-examined the drivers and outcomes of financial integration in Europe. Empirical analyses by Ganić (2020, 2021) provide new evidence on its structural determinants and distributional implications in post-transition and advanced European economies. The focus has been on questions about how effective financial integration has been achieved. As the book argues, the quality of financial integration is more important than its extent.

Fourth, regulatory harmonization has advantages (Lall, 2009), as the Basel framework seeks to establish common standards across jurisdictions. However, our research on the implementation of Basel II and Basel III across 100 countries shows large differences: the adoption rate is 18.2% in East Asia and the Pacific, compared to about 10% in Sub-Saharan Africa, Latin America, and the Caribbean. Results suggest that regulatory arbitrage remains an important part of the global financial system.

Fifth, our research shows that there are differences in the global financial cycle (Rey, 2013; Coimbra & Rey, 2017). Although the literature emphasizes that the global cycle drives capital flows, our analysis notes a high level of regional fragmentation. The Chinese corporate bond market no longer relies on the US cycle, and its beta coefficient has fallen to 0.28.

This suggests that in some cases, regional financial connectivity can reduce the market's exposure to global shocks.

In this book, we explore four key ideas that will help us better understand analysis in the following chapters. These ideas—rebalancing, resilience, competitive dynamics, and the role of crises as catalysts—form the foundation for understanding future structural changes in global finance. Each of these concepts encompasses specific changes taking place in global financial markets.

First, rebalancing: our international financial system is currently undergoing a significant structural crisis, which particularly affects major players such as the US, the European Union, and Japan.

Second, the resilience of a financial center or market refers to the ability to maintain competitive advantage and core functions during systemic shocks, as measured by GFCI stability, liquidity, and rapid recovery.

Third, competitive dynamics in assessing capital attractiveness include regulatory depth, technological advancement, geopolitical stability, and market size.

Fourth, regarding the catalysts of crises, the core idea is that severe economic shocks do not create new systems. Instead, they tend to simplify existing ones, expose vulnerabilities, and encourage their adaptability.

The book divides these issues into a few interrelated parts. Chapter 2 examines IFC's competitive advantages, building on the situational analysis in Chapter 3. Chapter 3 examines the development of global capital flows and financial integration in different regions from 2000 to 2023. Attention is paid to the structure of external assets and liabilities, as well as to the growing balance of payments between the United States, a net debtor, and the Asia Pacific, a stable net creditor. The results show that the stability of global shocks depends more on the level of financial integration than on any other factor. Chapter 4 reviews the history of the Basel Capital Accord, provides background analyses of Basel I, II, and III, and the proposals for Basel IV, and highlights differences in regulatory convergence across regions. Chapter 5 explores recent developments in the global FX markets and reviews trends in currency structures, instrument categories, and regional distribution. Chapter 6 examines the development of corporate debt, explores the growth of bond issuance from West to East, and analyzes regional patterns of concentration, dispersion, and instability. Chapter 7 investigates the flexibility, efficiency, breadth, and volatility of capital markets. Chapter 8 argues that serious financial crises create existing hierarchies, not new ones.

In short, the book is a persuasive, analytical evaluation of developments and transformations in the international financial system. There have been three key changes: the shift to multipolarity, the shift from banks to financial markets, and the integration of regional research and scholarly analysis on global financial cycles, regulatory convergence, and financial market risks.

## References

–Cassis, Y., & Wójcik, D. (2018). *International financial centres after the global financial crisis and Brexit*. Oxford University Press.

–Coimbra, N., & Rey, H. (2017). Financial cycles with heterogeneous intermediaries (CEPR Discussion Paper No. DP11907). https://cepr.org/publications/dp11907

–Farrell, H., & Newman, A.L. (2019). Weaponized interdependence: How global economic networks shape state coercion. *International Security*, 44(1), 42–79.

–Ganić, M. (2020). Are Determinants of International Financial Integration in the European Transition Countries Different from Post-Transition Countries? - Studies in Business and Economics. Volume: 15, Issue 1, 2020. https://doi.org/10.2478/sbe-2020-0005

–Ganić, M., Hrnjić, M. (2021). How Does International Financial Integration Really Affect Transition Countries' Growth? Empirical evidence from CEE-10 countries. The Journal of Central Banking Theory and Practice, Volume 10, Number 3. DOI: 10.2478/jcbtp-2021-0027.

Lall, R. (2009). *Why Basel II Failed and Why Any Basel III is Doomed*. Global Economic Governance Programme, University of Oxford.

–Lane, P.R. (2012). Financial globalization and the crisis (BIS Working Paper No.397). Bank for International Settlements, Monetary and Economic Department.

Lane, P. R., & Milesi-Ferretti, G. M. (2001). Vanjsko bogatstvo nacija: mjere strane imovine i obaveza za industrijske i zemlje u razvoju. *Journal of International Economics*, *55*(2), 263–294.

–Li, X. (2025). Conceptualizing China-US Rivalry through the Lens of Globalization in an Era of Changing Structure-Agency Dynamics. DOI: 10.1080/14747731.2025.2525037. https://www.tandfonline.com/doi/full/10.1080/14747731.2025.2525037#abstract

–Rey, H. (2013). Dilemma, not trilemma: The global financial cycle and monetary policy independence. In Global dimensions of unconventional monetary policy (pp. 285–333). Federal Reserve Bank of Kansas City.

–Starrs, S. K. (2019). Can China unmake the American making of global capitalism? Socialist Register, 55, 173–200.

–Winecoff, W. K. (2020). The persistent myth of lost hegemony, revisited: Structural power as a complex network phenomenon. *European Journal of International Relations*, 26(1), 209–252. https://doi.org/10.1177/1354066120952876

CHAPTER 2

# Global Finance in Transition: Competing Financial Centers

**Abstract** This chapter considers the development of IFCs and the transformation of the global financial geography by macroeconomic developments. Special focus is given to the growing power of the Asian world and the switch in the balance between conventional Western centers and newcomers. Also, the chapter centers on the multifaceted dynamics of international finance in three interacting aspects, namely, the evolution and operation of capital markets, the alteration of the competitive stance of major financial centers, and their capacity or inability to react to the current crisis. Data on debt market development, regional sector analysis, and OTC foreign exchange trading will illustrate the changes.

**Keywords** Capital market development • International financial centers (IFCs) • Global financial geography • OTC foreign exchange trading • Western vs. Asian financial hubs



M. Ganić, *Structural Change and Competitive Dynamics in Global Financial Markets*,
https://doi.org/10.1007/978-3-032-28906-3_2

## 2.1 Introduction

This chapter discusses the development of IFCs and the transformation of the global financial geography by macroeconomic developments. Special focus is given to the growing power of the Asian world and the switch in the balance between conventional Western centers and newcomers. Also, the chapter centers on the multifaceted dynamics of international finance in three interacting aspects, namely, the evolution and operation of capital markets, the alteration of the competitive stance of major financial centers, and their capacity or inability to react to the current crisis. Data on debt market development, regional sector analysis, and OTC foreign exchange trading will illustrate the changes.

The global financial landscape is undergoing rapid change, with significant redistribution of economic resources and growing competition among the world's most influential financial centers. Cassis (2016) argues that the transformation happens in two steps. The first is the globalization of the economy towards developing nations, including India and China. The second is the massive need for natural resources. With market liberalization and technological advances, existing International Financial Centers (IFCs) can expand and encourage the emergence of new ones.

This chapter explores three aspects of the development of the IFC that are interrelated in terms of crisis and support: (1) the growth of competition between old and new financial centers, (2) the structural evolution of the debt market as a source of resilience, and (3) the unequal influence of systemic issues, including the global financial crisis, COVID-19, and the war in Ukraine. The following argument is that crises do not establish new hierarchies. However, they merely simplify the state of affairs, enable the identification of structural vulnerabilities, and enhance flexibility.

## 2.2 Financial Structures Across Regions

The history of international debt issuance and the development of developed market economies were dissimilar. In the US, debt issuance is a significant source of funding for the private sector and government. Still, it has been observed only to expand in Canada, Japan, and most European nations over the past few decades. The international debt issuance arrangement is undergoing radical changes, with the most pronounced shifts by region (Kose et al., 2020).

**Table 2.1** Primary and secondary sources of financing structures by region (2023)

| *Region* | *Primary Financing Source* | *Secondary Source* |
|---|---|---|
| **United States** | Debt Capital Markets (74.9%) | Bank Lending (25.1%) |
| **Euro Area** | Bank Lending operations (80.7%) | Debt Capital Markets (19.3%) |
| **Japan** | Bank Lending operations (84.6%) | Debt Capital Markets (15.4%) |
| **China** | Bank Lending operations (68.2%) | Other (19.0%) |

Note: Euro-area = 20 EU member states that use the euro
Source: Author's elaboration on SIFMA fact book (2024). OECD, Federal Reserve, ECB, Bank of Japan, National Bureau of Statistics of China; SIFMA estimates

Table 2.1 illustrates the absence of a universal model of financing structures across regions. Every economic history and institution creates its own financial structure. Whereas the US (for example) values market efficiency and direct financing, Europe and Japan place greater emphasis on stability and long-term relationships through the banking system. China, however, uses its banking system to monitor the government's economic policy, while the broader financial sector expands in parallel.

The structure of corporate financing differs across leading economies, as shown in Table 2.1. In the US, 74.9% of financing for non-financial corporations (NFCs) comes from the debt securities market (DCM), while only 25.1% comes from bank loans. By comparison, the Eurozone, Japan, and China have high levels of indebtedness via bank credit, at 80.7%, 84.6%, and 68.2%, respectively.

The portion of the debt securities market (DCM) in total financing is 19.3% in the euro area, 15.4% in Japan, and 12.8% in China. In China, bank acceptances and foreign direct investment account for a large share of financing, comprising approximately 19.0% of total financing.

Global debt markets have experienced rapid growth and structural transformation in the last twenty-five years. For example, in 2024, the price of debt securities rose by 8% to almost $30 trillion, up from $5.4 trillion in 2000. Market growth varied and was influenced by sector-specific and regional factors.

As shown, the United Kingdom and the United States of America rank first as principal issuers, with outstanding debt of $3.56 trillion and $2.48 trillion, respectively (Table 2.2). The British market is bank-based, whereas the American market is dominated by other financial corporations,

**Table 2.2** Debt market development in leading financial centers (2024)

| *Financial Center* | *Total 2024 ($ Billions)* | *CAGR (2000–2024)* | *YoY Growth (2023–2024)* | *Market Share (2024)* | *Primary Growth Driver* |
|---|---|---|---|---|---|
| United States | 2,482.90 | 3.40% | 1.90% | 8.37% | Other Financial Corporations |
| United Kingdom | 3,562.90 | 7.10% | 3.50% | 12.01% | Banks |
| Germany | 1,336.00 | 6.00% | –1.20% | 4.50% | Other Fin. Corps. & Govt. |
| France | 1,290.00 | 6.60% | –3.90% | 4.35% | Government & NFCs |
| Japan | 517.2 | 6.90% | –0.70% | 1.74% | Banks |
| Canada | 1,344.50 | 8.10% | 4.60% | 4.53% | All Sectors |
| China | 250.1 | 13.40% | 7.90% | 0.84% | Broad-based expansion |
| Hong Kong SAR | 326.7 | 10.30% | –2.20% | 1.10% | Other Financial Corporations |
| India | 64.9 | 11.50% | –7.40% | 0.22% | Non-Financial Corporations |
| South Korea | 279.7 | 7.70% | 0.10% | 0.94% | Banks & NFCs |
| Subtotal (10 centers) | 11,454.90 | – | – | 38.60% | – |
| Other Markets | 18,209.30 | – | – | 61.40% | – |
| World Total | 29,664.20 | 7.60% | 3.10% | 100% | – |

Note: OFCs (financial institutions not central banks or deposit-taking banks, e.g., investment funds, insurance, and pension funds). NFCs (companies that produce goods/services, not financial mediation)
Source: Author's elaboration on BIS statistics (2024) data

indicating the emergence of a non-bank capital market. In 2024, both centers experienced stable growth (3.4% and 1.9%, respectively).

The rapid growth of Asian financial centers is a significant trend. China's compound annual growth rates (CAGR) are 10.3%, while those of Hong Kong and India are 11.5%. India is forecast to grow by 7.4% through 2024. With a CAGR of 4.6 % through 2024, the Canadian economy continues to grow. On the other hand, due to regional trends and reduced lending, France and Hong Kong are forecast to experience smaller declines in 2023–2024, of -3.9% and -2.2%, respectively.

Regional sector analysis data from BIS (2024) is shown in Fig. 2.1, which highlights significant changes in risk and funding patterns. The debt of OFCs (Other Financial Corporations) grew by 4.5% per year, while the debt of banks grew by 7% per year. In contrast, borrowing from non-financial corporations increased by only 0.4%, indicating that the financial sector was more active than the real economy. While Asian banks continued to expand lending, tighter regulations following the global financial crisis slowed the growth of bank debt in the West. The main financial centers have very different market structures. For instance, OFCs hold dominant positions in the advanced capital markets of the US and Hong Kong, with share percentages of 50.4% and 40.8%, respectively. In contrast, banking systems play a larger role in the UK and Japan, accounting for 44.8% and 57.2%, respectively. More than 57% of the Japanese market is controlled by banks (see Fig. 2.1).

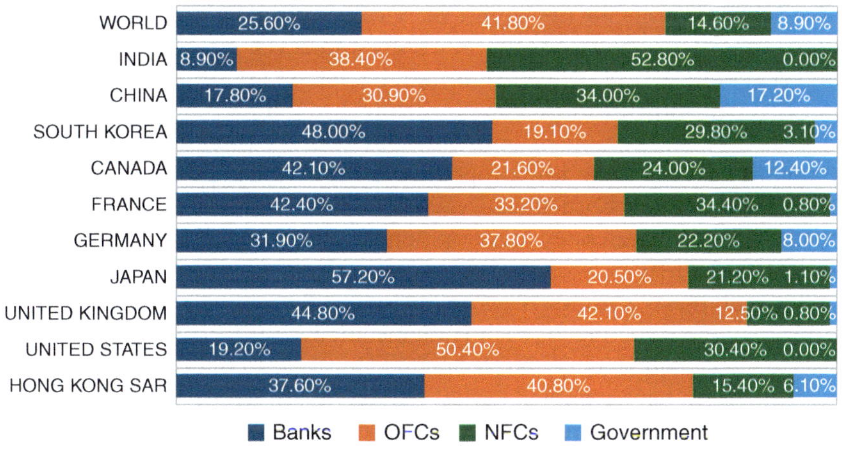


**Fig. 2.1** Sector analysis by issuer type (2024)
Note: The figure shows the distribution of large financial instruments by institution type across the major financial centers. OFCs are commonly referred to as investment funds, insurance companies, and pension funds. NFCs (Non-Financial Corporations) are companies that manufacture goods and services. National and local governments must be responsible. Deposit-taking institutions are banks. The figure might fail to capture 100 percent of the total of capital and other smaller categories
Source: Author's elaboration on BIS statistics (2024) data

Indeed, the US market is unique, with the ratio of non-financial corporate debt (30.4%) attesting to the well-developed state of corporate bonds and companies' direct access to market financing. Hong Kong's integration of robust OFC (40.8%) and banking services (37.6%) validates its status as Asia's largest international financial gateway (Fig. 2.1).

These balanced and diversified financial systems have been developed in some European countries, such as Germany and France, as well as in Canada, where the state and corporate sectors play important roles. France has the highest share of non-financial corporate debt in Europe (34.4%), indicating that companies rely heavily on the bond market. When we compare Canada with other developed countries, we notice that its debt-to-GDP ratio is 12.4%. On the other hand, in the Netherlands, banks and financial advisory companies record significantly higher debt ratios, at 31.9% and 37.8% respectively. Also, the projected share of the non-financial sector is 22.2%. In addition, the growth of emerging economies, such as India and China, plays a key role in shaping their debt structure. The NFC accounts for the largest share of India's debt structure (52.8%), illustrating the strong connection between financial market development and corporate activity. China, although buying a high proportion of NFC debt (34%), shows a more complex, state-conditioned model, with considerable representation of both the OFC market (30.9%) and the government (17.2%). The low proportion of traditional bank debt in both economies reflects both the diversified nature of financing sources and the particular, accelerated developmental process of Asian capital markets (Fig. 2.1).

Overall, there is no universal template for describing a global financial center, as the structure of each is determined by the economy's history, background, and level of development. Developed countries such as the United States have complex capital markets that include non-bank companies and differ from traditional systems that manage banks. In contrast, to stimulate real growth, companies are increasingly relying on corporate debt, as seen in emerging markets such as India (Patalano & Roulet, 2020). The functions of a global financial center vary with financial policy. However, the overall structure affects the distribution of financial risk and the likelihood that a financial shock will be transmitted to the entire economy.

## 2.3 The Evolving Landscape of IFCs

The financial services of IFCs originated in ancient trading cities of the Roman Empire and in centers of medieval Europe, including Genoa, Venice, and Constantinople, which had already contributed to trade by providing financial services. London had become a significant hub by the time of World War I, and trade and credit were dominated by private banks and ancient institutions such as the Banco Vanco della Piazza de Rialto (Venice, 1584) and the Amsterdam Stock Exchange (1602). IFCs began to expand in the foreign exchange market, the European capital market, and offshore centers, becoming centers of capital, talent, and financial infrastructure between the 1950s and the 1980s. With the advent of globalization and the emergence of transnational financial intermediaries in the 1980s, IFCs came to the heart of global investment, banking, and financial systems (Sidenko, 2021).

Despite the significant role that IFCs play in global economic decision-making, their status and location remain unclear. While these connections will help us understand the mechanisms of interaction and transformation of IFCs (Derudder et al., 2011; Lai et al., 2020), it remains unclear where power resides and how it is transferred across IFC boundaries. The focus on analyzing and planning the functions of IFCs has led to a lack of understanding of how they connect financial systems and of the asymmetric power relations that arise from these connections (Wójcik et al., 2022).

The competition between the United States and China is a subject on which scholars have varied opinions. Winecoff (2020) adds that the United States remains a critical part of global finance despite China's rapid growth and the increasing level of transnational relations. On the other hand, Schindler et al. (2024) examine the impact of the US-China rivalry across four major global networks: infrastructure, digital systems, manufacturing, and finance.

They conclude that, since most parties prefer to unite with larger powers, no single power can absolutely dominate. Starrs (2019) assumes that China's development occurs as a global capitalist machine, largely dependent on the United States. For example, a future China will disengage from current global problems rather than self-isolate.

The GFC and the COVID-19 pandemic have not only destabilized and disrupted markets but also dictated how markets operate and enabled a new generation of leaders to assume leadership positions. To understand the contemporary global financial market and its major players, it is necessary to consider crises in terms of the factors that caused them.

Over the past decade, global financial markets have undergone significant changes. These changes have often been triggered by extreme crises, such as the GFC and COVID-19. They have not only caused instability but also acted as catalysts, amplifying existing trends and forcing market participants to react quickly to changing conditions. In addition, this is a major transformation of market fundamentals. Traditional financial centers, including key ones, remain important. However, emerging markets are playing an increasingly prominent role, especially in the Asia-Pacific region, where China is becoming a global financial power. Many studies examining the development and role of Asian IFCs use this approach (e.g., Lai, 2018; Meyer, 2018; Pan et al., 2016). IFCs in Asia often perform complementary functions within the IFC framework, which distinguishes them from other IFC structures. Karreman and Van der Knaap (2012) found that the location of initial public offerings (IPOs) in China shows increasing specialization and functional compatibility, which positively affects cooperation among Asian IFC networks. However, there is also competition among the Hong Kong, Singapore, and Shanghai hubs. This competition is explained by threats to their local advantages, policies, and organizational structures in attracting foreign companies (Jarvis, 2011). At the same time, the funding process is also shifting. For example, as businesses increasingly issue bonds and become less dependent on bank lending, the regulatory environment has become tougher after each crisis; Basel III, following the GFC, is an example. Moreover, the global corporate debt-to-GDP ratio has been steadily increasing, further defining the market.

These alterations directly affect the nature of competition. The traditional participants lose some of the influence they previously gained: European banks and American bond issuers, whereas new players are becoming increasingly active: Asian corporations and states and Middle Eastern sovereign wealth funds. Meanwhile, emerging financial centers in cities such as Singapore and Hong Kong are beginning to challenge the older financial centers of power, New York and London. Lastly, crises have a catalytic effect—they do not bring change out of nothing but rather speed up trends that already exist and make them more noticeable and rampant.

Two fundamental transformations of the recent past can explain the latest development of IFCs worldwide. On the one hand, the economy and workplaces are gradually becoming oriented toward developing countries, at least toward China and India (and possibly others). Secondly, unprecedented demand for the world's natural resources has emerged, with the Middle East and Russia as the main suppliers, along with some Latin American countries. These transformations have opened the gate to what could be considered the most significant redistribution of wealth and economic dynamism in history. Simultaneously, this transition has been precipitated by the liberalization of trade policy in the area, leading to a reduction in capital expenditure (Cassis, 2016).

Recent years have seen emerging Asian financial centers particularly assert their status as global centers. However, they still primarily cover investment banking, insurance services, OTC derivatives, interest rate futures, and equity index futures, as traditional powerhouses such as New York and London do (Le Leslé et al., 2014). This implies a change in the geography of international finance, as established Western financiers share the stage with new, emerging big players in developing countries, all operating on an increasingly global financial platform. The same trends were observed in the OTC foreign exchange market, where the United Kingdom recorded the highest share of global turnover in 2019 at 43%, and by 2025, its daily turnover reached $4.75 trillion—a 27% increase from 2022 (Fig. 2.2).

These ratings confirm London and New York's continued leadership and demonstrate the growing influence of Asia on global currency markets.[1]

The U.S. remains the second-largest FX center in the world, with turnover growing at an annual rate of 2.34–2.37 trillion through 2019. This expansion further reinforces London's and New York's positions in the global FX market. The growth of Asian centers is also remarkable: Singapore is developing the fastest, with a 59.8% growth rate, and its turnover is rising as well, making it, as a result, the third-largest global center, with $640 billion in 2019 and $1.49 trillion in 2025. Hong Kong, at $883 billion, and Japan, at $440 billion, are also increasing, albeit slowly. Germany is the most rapidly expanding hub in Europe, in percentage terms with turnover projected to reach $386 billion by 2025, up from $124 billion in 2019 (Fig. 2.2).

[1] Please see Chapter 5 for a comprehensive analysis of the structure of the currency market, the set of instruments traded, and regional trends.

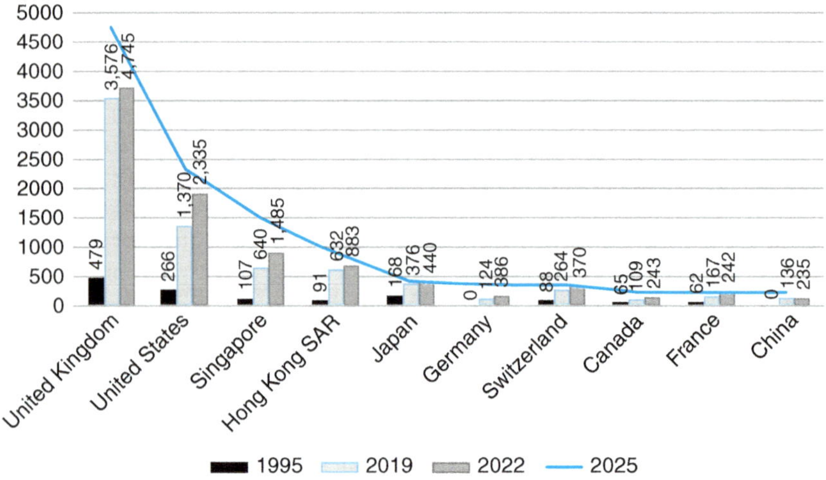


**Fig. 2.2** Global FX turnover by region (daily averages in $ billion)
Source: Author's elaboration on data for 1995, 2019, 2022, and 2025 from the BIS Triennial Survey

Switzerland maintains its long-standing presence as a stable global hub, reaching $370 billion in 2025. Canada and France are also experiencing strong growth, recording turnovers of $243 billion and $242 billion, respectively. China is also among the Top 10 countries, confirming its growing role in FX markets, with daily turnover increasing from $136 billion in 2019 to $235 billion in 2025. In 2025, the top ten countries in the world generated $11.36 trillion in daily trading, accounting for 90.4% of the world market. For example, in 2019, the remaining countries accounted for $2.88 trillion, or 34.8% of global market share, and by 2025, their overall share had decreased to $1.26 trillion, or 9.6% of global market share, indicating that OTC foreign exchange instrument trading is increasingly concentrated in the major financial centers (Fig. 2.2).

## 2.4 Global Financial Centers in Crisis and Recovery

The so-called world cities, the central and most successful cities, have become IFCs and the main hubs of global competition and reciprocal competition in various areas. As globalization accelerates, financial services are becoming increasingly global, and access to capital, coupled with sophisticated financial engineering methods, is becoming more transparent, further increasing the importance of major financial centers.

The eight leading global financial centers in the run-up to the GFC were New York, London, Tokyo, Frankfurt, Paris, Hong Kong, Singapore, and Zurich (with Geneva) (Cassis, 2010). After a decade, the top eight cities remained in the same order, though Frankfurt and Paris had overtaken some of them, and Tokyo had done so to a lesser extent. Moreover, a new challenger was also introduced to the list: Shanghai (with Beijing advancing in significance). On the surface, it may seem that the most serious financial crisis in modern history had little impact on the status quo of the international order (Cassis & Wojcik, 2018). Another notable example is the Brexit referendum in June 2016, which was one of the most impactful political and economic events of the past 10 years yet failed to visibly shift the locations of the biggest centers.

Nevertheless, the main concern is the impact of COVID-19 on key global financial institutions and regions worldwide. Li and Zhao (2018) stated that government estimates were frequently based on authoritative publications such as the annual Banker and the Global Funds Financial Center Index (GFCI). According to the GFCI definition, a financial center is a place where major global financial transactions and operations occur (Z/Yen Group & China Development Institute, 2025).

The COVID-19 crisis is the first significant challenge to the global financial system since the G20 reforms that followed the 2008 crisis (Financial Stability Board, 2021). In contrast to the economic crisis, the pandemic has taught valuable lessons about future policy and the operation of the regulatory reforms. The introduced reforms and sound policy measures made the system more resilient to the pandemic than it was in 2008. Big banks were better capitalized, liquidated, and less leveraged; central counterparty infrastructures operated in a stable environment. However, in March of 2020, the weaknesses became clear: major funding markets were under strain, and authorities needed to intervene swiftly and at scale to maintain stability and provide liquidity and support to the real economy (FSB, 2021).

A comparative overview of the crisis periods (2019, 2022, and 2024) indicates that the most developed world financial centers (New York, London, and Hong Kong) maintained stability during the COVID-19 pandemic (Table 2.3).

In essence, the COVID-19 pandemic has accelerated existing trends. One example is the emergence of successful crisis management in the

**Table 2.3** Comparative overview through crisis periods (2019 vs. 2022 vs. 2024)

| *Region& IFC* | *GFCI 25 (2019) Pre-Crises* | *GFCI 31 (2022) During/ post-Crisis* | *GFCI 37 (2024) Current rank change* | *Change (2019 vs. 2024)* | *Impact of crisis/Trend* |
|---|---|---|---|---|---|
| **Global top 5 IFCs** | | | | | |
| New York | 1 | 1 | 1 | 0 | demonstrated good stability during the COVID-19 pandemic |
| London | 2 | 2 | 2 | 0 | |
| Hong Kong | 3 | 3 | 3 | 0 | |
| Singapore | 4 | 6 | 4 | 0 | returning to the old position after a temporary fall. |
| Tokyo | 5 | 9 | 22 | −17 | experienced the steepest decline, reflecting a loss of competitiveness. |
| **Western Europe** | | | | | |
| Frankfurt | 10 | 15 | 11 | −1 | A slight decline, but stable. |
| Paris | 24 | 22 | 17 | 7 | Achieved continued growth, with post-Brexit gains. |
| Amsterdam | 36 | 28 | 18 | 18 | made a significant gain, attracting business that previously took place in London. |
| **Eastern Europe & Central Asia** | | | | | |
| Warszawa | 61 | 50 | 101 | −40 | Hard hit by the war in Ukraine. |
| Moscow | 62 | 73 | N/A | N/A | The effect of sanctions was eliminated from the list. |
| Istanbul | 79 | 81 | 107 | −28 | Ongoing inflationary and currency difficulties. |
| **The Middle East** | | | | | |
| Dubai | 12 | 17 | 12 | 0 | Great resistance. It went back to the pre-crisis level. |

| | | | | | |
|---|---|---|---|---|---|
| Abu Dhabi | 35 | 35 | 38 | –3 | Moderately resistant to the impact of the crisis |
| **Asia and the Pacific** | | | | | |
| Hong Kong | 3 | 3 | 3 | 0 | It holds third place, which proves its strength. |
| Singapore | 4 | 6 | 4 | 0 | Singapore has been resilient, remaining right behind Hong Kong and never leaving the top five. |
| Tokyo | 5 | 9 | 22 | -17 | experienced the steepest decline |
| Shanghai | 19 | 4 | 8 | 11 | the successful crisis management |
| Shenzhen | 22 | 9 | 9 | 13 | the successful crisis management |
| Seoul | 28 | 10 | 10 | 18 | Significant progress. |
| **North America** | | | | | |
| New York | 1 | 1 | 1 | no changes | Complete stability on top. The impact of the crisis was minimal. Dominance is even increasing. |
| San Francisco | 6 | 8 | 5 | 1 | Clear winner. The technology and venture capital sectors are booming during and after the pandemic. |
| Chicago | 9 | 10 | 6 | 3 | Steady progress. Coming together as a varied financial center. |
| Los Angeles | 14 | 11 | 7 | 7 | Significant rise. Exploited remote employment and talent acquisition. |
| Toronto | 13 | 12 | 23 | –10 | The biggest loser in the region. Probably lost short-term benefit in the pandemic. |

Source: Author's comparison based on The Global Financial Centers Index centers of China (Shanghai and Shenzhen) and South Korea (Seoul). Another example is Tokyo's stagnation (Z/Yen Group & China Development Institute, 2025). On the other hand, the war in Ukraine has significantly reduced the perception of insecurity in the region, as evidenced by its large impacts. It led to the immediate removal of Moscow from the financial system. Paris and Amsterdam have emerged as viable alternatives, despite the energy crisis having a negligible impact on Central European cities like Frankfurt.

Therefore, crises do not introduce new tendencies; they only increase existing ones. Global shocks are accelerators, and geopolitical conflicts are the immediate and disastrous effects on perceived risk in vulnerable areas.

The war in Ukraine and the energy crisis have exposed clear winners and losers within the European financial landscape. While key international financial hubs, such as Frankfurt and Zurich, have experienced a slight decline, likely due to the war's indirect economic impact, Paris and Amsterdam have continued their gradual growth. Geopolitical uncertainty in the East has further solidified their role as havens for international capital, reinforcing the perception that they represent a stable and reliable European alternative to London after Brexit.

During the analysis of the crisis, North America, and in particular the United States, emerged as a dominant force in the global financial system. While other parts of the world were going through difficult times, all major American cities—New York, San Francisco, Chicago, Los Angeles, and Boston—managed to maintain or even improve their positions (see Table 2.3).

Between 2022 and 2024, their ratings rose significantly.

The pandemic has brought some changes. Capital is returning to the US as a safe investment, while some domestic economic issues have reduced Toronto's appeal. Although Tokyo is lagging, key Asian cities such as Shanghai, Shenzhen, and Seoul have shown remarkable resilience and improved their performance since the beginning of the COVID-19 pandemic (Z/Yen Group & China Development Institute, 2025). This growth was recorded in GFCI 29, suggesting that the region has successfully managed the crisis and experienced a rapid economic recovery, thereby gaining significant global trust as a center.

The comparative analysis of the GFCI between the pre-pandemic (2019–2021), post-pandemic, and current (2024) periods reveals a landscape of both stability and significant shift (Table 2.4).

This illustrates that the COVID-19 pandemic has caused a truly universal crisis, leading to different recovery trajectories around the world. The four largest financial centers—New York, London, Hong Kong, and Singapore—have maintained their leading positions, but all have fallen in the rankings during the pandemic. The largest declines were recorded in London (-44 points) and Hong Kong (-42 points) (see Table 2.4). Each of these centers experienced a sharp decline between 2019 and 2021. For example, London was hit by the combined effects of Brexit and COVID-19, while Hong Kong suffered from political unrest and strict lockdowns. However, when we look at the long-term figures from 2019 to 2025, the global financial system is in permanent decline, and macroeconomic uncertainty is increasing. Namely, none of these centers has returned to pre-crisis levels. The differences became even more noticeable after the crisis: London and Hong Kong again found themselves in the plus (each gained 19 points from 2021), and Singapore continues its development (gained 10 points), while New York confirmed its leadership (gained 5 points).

Shanghai and Tokyo, unfortunately, ended up as losers in this story. Shanghai is facing a difficult recovery and various geopolitical and regulatory obstacles, resulting in a net rating drop of 26 points. Tokyo fell 16 places in the ranking, and this can be directly linked to the same rating drop, making it the largest absolute loser among the world's metropolises (see Table 2.4).

**Table 2.4** GFCI Evolution of leading IFCs (2019 vs. 2024)

| *Financial Center* | *GFCI 37 (2025)* | *GFCI 25 (2019)* | *GFCI 29 (2021)* | *Rank Change (2019–2025)* | *Rating Change (2019–2025)* | *Pandemic Impact (2019–2021)* | *Recovery (2021–2025)* |
|---|---|---|---|---|---|---|---|
| New York | 1 (769) | 1 (794) | 1 (764) | 0 | –25 | –30 | 5 |
| London | 2 (762) | 2 (787) | 2 (743) | 0 | –25 | –44 | 19 |
| Hong Kong | 3 (760) | 3 (783) | 4 (741) | 0 | –23 | –42 | 19 |
| Singapore | 4 (750) | 4 (772) | 5 (740) | 0 | –22 | –32 | 10 |
| Shanghai | 8 (744) | 5 (770) | 3 (742) | –3 | –26 | –28 | 2 |
| Tokyo | 22 (730) | 6 (756) | 7 (736) | –16 | –26 | –20 | -6 |

Source: Author's comparison based on The Global Financial Centers Index

In this chapter, we expand on the current debate about the role of the International Financial Center (IFC), which was initiated by Cassis and Wojcik in 2018. Our analysis shows that, while research suggests cities often exhibit resilience in times of crisis, this resilience may be masked by deeper structural problems. The GFCI ratings clearly show that cities like New York, London, and Hong Kong have not suffered serious consequences. Our review of debt markets illustrates how these cities have managed to hold up thanks to the flexibility of their regulatory frameworks, the diversity of their markets, and their favorable geopolitical positions.

## 2.5 Conclusion

The modern global financial market has become more resilient, more competitive, and, it seems, more prone to rapid reactions to crises. It is no longer just one-sided; it is now multipolar, and the old power centers like New York and London are no longer the only players, although they still have deep market roots, excellent infrastructure, and stability.

Asian financial centers, such as Hong Kong and Singapore, are now at the forefront, as their access to global capital and specialized services enables them to challenge traditional hierarchies. According to research by Petrakis et al. (2025), although the GFC, the COVID-19 pandemic, and the economic crisis in Ukraine have brought about significant changes, they have not created new trends but have only accelerated those that were already in place.

These events have led to obvious structural differences, such as the sudden decline of Tokyo and the sanctions that hit Moscow. On the other hand, many cities, such as San Francisco, Shanghai, and Amsterdam, have shown remarkable resilience, stability, and predictability. Today, the position of the IFC depends on a complex combination of factors: regulatory flexibility, technological innovation, geopolitical security, and the depth of the financial sector. The future would be marked by increasing rivalry between the East and the West, as well as among talent hubs in fintech, green finance, and private wealth management. The most characteristic figure of the new global finance is not the deterioration of old centers with the emergence of new ones but the transformation into a compound, interlinked, and highly competitive network in which stability and imagination become the most valuable currency.

## References


–Bank for International Settlements. (2022). Turnover of over-the-counter foreign exchange instruments: Daily averages in April 2022 (Triennial Central Bank Survey). https://www.bis.org/statistics/rpfx22_fx.pdf

–Bank for International Settlements (2024). International debt securities issues and amounts outstanding (BIS-compiled). BIS Statistics.

–Bank for International Settlements. (2025). Turnover of over-the-counter foreign exchange instruments: Daily averages in April 2025, OTC foreign exchange turnover in April 2025, Triennial Central Bank Survey.

–Cassis, Y. (2010). *Capitals of capital: The rise and fall of international financial centers*. Cambridge University Press.

–Cassis, Y. (2016). International financial centers after the global financial crisis and Brexit. Oxford University Press.

–Cassis, Y., & Wójcik, D. (Eds.). (2018). International financial centers after the global financial crisis and Brexit. Oxford University Press. https://doi.org/10.1093/oso/9780198817314.001.0001

–Derudder, B., Hoyler, M., & Taylor, P. (2011). Goodbye Reykjavik: International banking centers and the global financial crisis. Area, 43(2), 173–182. https://doi.org/10.1111/j.1475-4762.2010.00968.x

–Financial Stability Board - FSB (2021, July 13). Lessons learned from the COVID-19 pandemic from a financial stability perspective: Interim report. https://www.fsb.org/2021/07/lessons-learnt-from-the-covid-19-pandemic-from-a-financial-stability-perspective-interim-report/

–Jarvis, D. (2011). Race for the money: International financial centers in Asia. Journal of International Relations and Development, 14, 60–95. https://doi.org/10.2139/ssrn.1413524

–Karreman, B., & van der Knaap, B. (2012). The geography of equity listing and financial center competition in mainland China and Hong Kong. Journal of Economic Geography, 12(4), 899–922. https://doi.org/10.1093/jeg/lbr015

–Kose, M. A., Nagle, P. S. O., Ohnsorge, F. L., & Sugawara, N. (2020). Can this time be different? Policy options in times of rising debt (World Bank Policy Research Working Paper No. 9178). World Bank. http://hdl.handle.net/10986/33427

–Lai, K. (2018). Singapore: Connecting Asian markets with global finance. In Y. Cassis & D. Wójcik (Eds.), International financial centers after the global financial crisis and Brexit (pp. 154–181). Oxford University Press.

–Lai, K., Pan, F., Sokol, M., & Wójcik, D. (2020). New financial geographies of Asia. *Regional Studies*, *54*(2), 143–148. https://doi.org/10.1080/00343404.2019.1689549

–Le Leslé, V., Ohnsorge, F. L., Kim, M., & Seshadri, S. (2014). Why complementarity matters for stability—Hong Kong SAR and Singapore as Asian financial centers (IMF Working Paper No. 14/119). International Monetary Fund. https://doi.org/10.5089/9781498334464.001

–Li, C. L. K., & Zhao, S. X. (2018). The rise of international financial centers in bank-based and market-based financial systems. Banks and Banking Systems, 13(4), 161–172. https://doi.org/10.21511/bbs.13(4).2018.15
–Meyer, D. (2018). Hong Kong, Shanghai, and Beijing: China's contenders for global financial center leadership. In Y. Cassis & D. Wójcik (Eds.), International financial centers after the global financial crisis and Brexit. Oxford University Press.
–Pan, F., Zhao, S., & Wójcik, D. (2016). The rise of venture capital centers in China: A spatial and network analysis. Geoforum, 75, 148–158. https://doi.org/10.1016/j.geoforum.2016.07.013
–Patalano, R., & Roulet, C. (2020). Structural developments in global financial intermediation: The rise of debt and non-bank credit intermediation (OECD Working Papers on Finance, Insurance and Private Pensions No. 44). OECD Publishing. https://dx.doi.org/10.1787/daa87f13-en
–Petrakis, P. E., Vasilis, G., & Kanzola, A.-M. (2025). Social Megatrends. In Palgrave Studies in the Future of European Societies and Economies (pp. 239–268). Springer Nature. https://doi.org/10.1007/978-3-031-86437-7_11
–Schindler, S., Alami, I., DiCarlo, J., Jepson, N., Rolf, S., Bayırbağ, M. K., Cyuzuzo, L., DeBoom, M., Farahani, A. F., Liu, I. T., & McNicol, H. (2024). The second cold war: US-China competition for centrality in infrastructure, digital. Production and Finance Networks. Geopolitics, 29(4), 1083–1120.
–Securities Industry and Financial Markets Association. (2024). SIFMA Capital Markets Fact Book 2024 https://www.sifma.org/resources/research/statistics/fact-book/
–Sidenko, S. (2021). International financial centers in the global economy. Finance Economics & Education, 6(4), 37. https://doi.org/10.30525/2500-946X/2021-4-6 http://baltijapublishing.lv/index.php/econedu/article/view/1590
–Starrs, S. K. (2019). Can China unmake the American making of global capitalism? Socialist Register, 55, 173–200.
–Winecoff, W. K. (2020). The persistent myth of lost hegemony revisited: Structural power as a complex-network phenomenon. European Journal of International Relations, 26(1), 209–252. https://doi.org/10.1177/1354066120952876
–Wójcik, D., Keenan, L., Pažitka, V., Urban, M., & Wu, W. (2022). The changing landscape of international financial centers in the twenty-first century: Cross-border mergers and acquisitions in the global financial network. Economic Geography, 98(2), 97–118. https://doi.org/10.1080/00130095.2021.2010535
–Z/Yen Group & China Development Institute. (2025). Global Financial Centers Index 37. https://www.longfinance.net/documents/GFCI_37_Report_2025.03.20_v1.2.pd

CHAPTER 3

# Capital Flows and Financial Integration: A Study of Global and Regional Markets

**Abstract** The chapter offers an insight into the modern international financial environment. The chapter proceeds to an empirical study of 45 countries from 2000 to 2023, emphasizing the composition of external assets and liabilities and the disequilibrium between capital exporters and importers. It also explores the relationship between the main world regions on opposite sides of global foreign investment imbalances: capital-exporting nations, which invest abroad, and capital-importing countries, which rely on foreign inflows. Chapter 3 ends on a cautionary note: alternative development may pose a risk to global financial market stability, particularly in a high-interest-rate environment.

**Keywords** Capital flows • External assets and liabilities • Financial integration • Global financial imbalances • Crisis resilience (GFC and COVID-19)



M. Ganić, *Structural Change and Competitive Dynamics in Global Financial Markets*,
https://doi.org/10.1007/978-3-032-28906-3_3

## 3.1 Introduction

As described in the introduction, the surge in international capital movements in the 1980s changed external balance sheets as measured in this section. The crucial players in international financial markets are now MNCs and large-scale conglomerates operating worldwide (Broner et al., 2013). Thus, the business focused more on pursuing more profitable investments rather than engaging in productive activities. Additionally, in the 1970s, oil prices soared, causing petrodollars to circulate rapidly through the banking system. Moreover, interdependencies among financial entities such as commercial and investment banks, brokerages, and others are becoming increasingly intense and global. So, businesses sought more profitable investment opportunities than the productive sphere offered.

The modern financial system can be described as the integration of capital markets and international investors, a process that accelerated in the 1980s. Some empirical research indicates a correlation between economic integration and business cycle trends (Imbs, 2004; Kose et al., 2003; Kalemli-Ozcan et al., 2009). According to Schularick and Steger (2006), capital market liberalization was a significant source of growth in the past. As a result of this close relationship between the EU, the US, and Japan, Bencivenga and Smith (1991) predicted additional integration of financial markets. In the 1980s, the first waves of financial integration took shape after barriers to capital flows were removed, as investors sought higher yields and an environment for international risk diversification was established. Capital market integration has been accompanied by a significant rise in cross-border integration of portfolio assets and liabilities and, to a lesser extent, through FDI, bank loans, and deposits.

It is a panel that includes 45 countries from 2000 to 2023 and is divided into four regions: the Americas, Europe, Asia Pacific, and Africa. It offers an in-depth analysis of foreign assets and liabilities, including direct investment, portfolio equity, and debt. All the figures are calculated on balance-of-payments data gathered by the IMF and the 2024 Milesi-Ferretti report. The assets and liabilities are recorded at the end of each year and converted to dollars at the exchange rate that existed then. In contrast, GDP and flows are translated using the average annual exchange rate. This chapter also explores the interactions among regions worldwide that lie at opposite ends of the global foreign investment imbalance: one group of nations that export capital and another that imports it.

## 3.2 The Great Rebalancing

Increasing evidence shows that the world financial architecture is structured so that the leading player, the United States, competes with several major creditor economies, particularly in developed Asia and Europe (Milesi-Ferretti, 2023). In this respect, persistent international disparities in portfolio equity and investment have significantly shaped global capital flows. Furthermore, they are among the primary structural factors that led to the global economic meltdown and to the existence of the American system of managed deficits (Obstfeld & Rogoff, 2009). Systemically, the effective operation of the global economy is usually tied to the quality of the transfer of surplus capital from other nations to the United States through financial markets. These fiscal markets effectively finance the world's deficit and keep the world's macroeconomy balanced (Varoufakis, 2015).

As noted earlier, rebalancing refers to the structural pressures of the global financial system on Asia and the Pacific. Based on experience, unexpected fluctuations in exchange rates and asset prices significantly affect the valuation of net foreign assets. This has a direct impact on the price of capital, the country's borrowing capacity, and the real economy, particularly investment (Gertler et al., 2007; Ghironi et al., 2015; Caballero, 2021).

The key portfolios for evaluating a nation's external asset structure are equity, foreign direct investment, debt, and financial derivatives. These classifications provide an operational overview of a nation's holdings abroad. Thus, we compare these indicators across world regions. There have been significant shifts in the composition of external assets over the last twenty years (Ganić, 2020). Although debt had been the major contributor in the entire 2000–2008 period (49.7% average), a promising shift towards portfolio equity and foreign direct investment (FDI) began in 2016, and it looks promising as it takes the lead in providing 51.4% of the total external asset composition by 2023 (Fig. 3.1).

Such a transition signifies a shift in the valuation of risk and national balance sheets. Europe and the Asia Pacific have capitalized on this trend to become more resistant to their creditors. At the same time, the United States has given up part of its stability to gain liquidity. Africa is almost entirely dependent on FDI. While this may appear to be a hedge, the continent's small market size is only $0.83 trillion, making it highly susceptible to a drastic inversion in capital flows. The Americas have experienced a notable shift in their external asset portfolio, moving from a focus on FDI

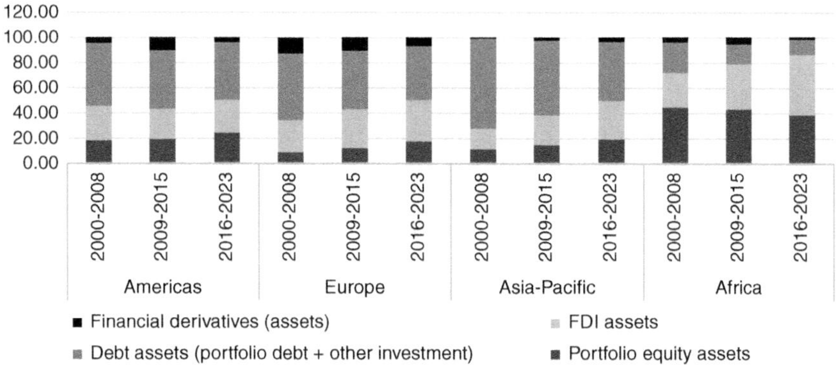


**Fig. 3.1** Change in the composition of external assets by region (2000–2023)
Notes: **The Americas** include Argentina, Brazil, Canada, Chile, Costa Rica, Mexico, and the United States.
**Europe** includes Austria, Belgium, Bulgaria, Croatia, Cyprus, the Czech Republic, Denmark, Finland, France, Germany, Greece, Hungary, Ireland, Italy, Luxembourg, Malta, the Netherlands, Norway, Poland, Portugal, Romania, Russia, the Slovak Republic, Slovenia, Spain, Sweden, Switzerland, Turkey, and the United Kingdom.
**Asia Pacific** includes Australia, China, Hong Kong, India, Japan, South Korea, New Zealand, Pakistan, and the Philippines.
**Africa** includes South Africa.
Source: Author's calculation on Milesi-Ferretti (2024) data

(27.5% in 2000–2008) to a greater emphasis on portfolio equity investments (26.2% in 2016–2023), with a rising focus on market-liquidated assets. Also, it alludes to the fact that before the GFC, external portfolios in the Americas were dominated by FDI and debt (approximately 73% of external asset composition).

Canada and Brazil devoted 52% and 64% of their foreign direct investment to the real economy. In contrast, Mexico and Costa Rica, with 55% and 82% of their debt, had to depend more on fixed-income instruments. The U.S. foreign assets are split equally between direct and long-term investments, each at 36% (data for individual countries are sourced from Milesi-Ferretti, 2024). This trend was interrupted by the GFC, during which derivatives accounted for 32% of America's total external asset composition and were used to hedge institutional interests.

During the GFC, derivatives increased temporarily as a share of total external assets (10.7% in the 2009–2015 period) to hedge risk but have since declined (Fig. 3.1). Following the GFC, the Americas became more liquidity- and risk-protection-oriented. The rate of equity investments also rose regionally from 15% to 19%, driven by promising economic conditions stemming from quantitative easing policies. Especially, the U.S. (24%) and Chile (39%) saw equity shares in total external assets exceed the regional average. Derivatives have become a significant risk-management tool, with an average of 18% of U.S. external assets and a maximum of 5.7% in Mexico. The share of FDI in total external assets generally declines, except in Brazil (71%). Although debt remains the dominant segment of external assets in the Americas region (45–50%), it has decreased slightly by 4.6 percentage points. In addition, the equity share increased by 6.2 percentage points. Given the Americas region's status as a net debtor, this increases exposure to capital markets and financial risk (Fig. 3.1). However, a new portfolio structure emerged between 2016 and 2023, with FDI rising to 24.3% of total external assets in the Americas.

The USA, Chile, and Canada performed exceptionally well, with FDI shares in total external assets of 33%, 38%, and 31%, respectively. In the meantime, Costa Rica experienced an increase in FDI shares of external assets from 18.6% to 19%. Brazil was also doing well, increasing its foreign direct investment to an incredible 77%, while Argentina remains heavily reliant on debt at 75%.

Regarding derivatives, they are stabilizing their shares at 4.5% of external assets, except in Mexico, where it is 6.2%. The US has a highly mature, market-oriented asset structure with an increasing focus on equities and derivatives. This change is indicative of increased returns and improved risk management.

This naturally follows its position as a world financial hub. Despite this decrease in debt assets, it could not offset the steep rise in liabilities, thereby worsening the net financial position (NFA).

Between 2000 and 2023, Europe has experienced a significant transformation in its portfolio. The proportion of FDI has risen, and the debt level has declined from 57.9% (2000–2008) to 42.2% (2016–2023). Derivatives emerged as the key risk-management instrument, increasing by 6.8 percentage points during the GFC, from 4.5% to 11.3% of total external liabilities, although their share later moderated to 7.6% (Fig. 3.1). The reforms made Europe much more credible as a creditor and reduced its exposure to interest-rate fluctuations. In the 2000s, 55% of external assets were recorded as debt, with Bulgaria at 96% and Greece at 85%. The level of FDI was between 25% and 30%, and equity investments ranged from 13% to 24%, with Norway at 25% and Sweden at 24%. (Data from Milesi-Ferretti, 2024).

A major change in the structure of Europe's external assets occurred after 2008, when the shift towards debt instruments was gradually reversed. FDI emerged as the main external asset category in the first period of rebalancing (2009–2015), with Hungary (85%) and Cyprus (83%) showing extreme levels of concentration, while regional debt fell to 48%. Simultaneously, the UK retained a remarkable exposure to derivatives (>25%), while Germany created its own derivative market (13%). At the more modern stage (2016–2023), Europe has moved to a balanced diversification strategy: equity has been reinforced (average 17%), particularly in the Nordic countries, with Norway (52%) and Finland (33%) recording the highest shares globally. FDI is now at a stabilized level of about 32%, and the debt has further decreased to 42% of the external assets. The progress, however, is uneven, as Greece and Romania continue to have high levels of debt dependence (>60%). Consequently, the Nordic countries currently hold the world's most advanced portfolios, as over half of their foreign assets are invested in equities (country-level data are obtained from the original Milesi-Ferretti dataset, 2024).

The Asia Pacific has shifted its debt-dominated portfolio (69.7% in 2000–2008) by 2016–2023, with FDI and portfolio equity accounting for half of the external assets. Entry into international value chains produced a 15 pp increase in FDI (to 31% of external asset composition), an increase in equity (from 11.5% to 19.1%), and a 23 pp reduction in debt to 46.5%. Derivatives remained low (below 4% of external assets), suggesting that resilience stems from actual diversification rather than financial insurance (Fig. 3.1). Some countries, such as Pakistan (86%), China (83%), and the Philippines (80%), had the highest debt levels in the early 2000s. In comparison, Australia and India had the highest FDI rates at 42% each, whereas portfolio equity had the smallest share at 11%.

Derivatives were marginal (below 2% of external assets) except in Australia (7%) and New Zealand (9%). Advanced economies had more balanced portfolios than emerging markets, which were heavily indebted. FDI was prioritized (32%) after 2008, and portfolio equity grew to 13%. Several countries in the region, such as India, the Philippines, and China, have recorded high growth of FDI investments. In contrast, Korea and Japan, among others, have been raising capital through internal reforms designed to restructure their home countries' economies. The share of portfolio equity in total external assets rose to 17% (reaching 41% in New Zealand, 26% in Korea, and 29% in Australia); FDI rose to 32% (45% in China and 51% in Philippines); and the share of debt in external assets dropped to 47%, though it remained high in Pakistan and Hong Kong (>75%), according to the latest phase (the data on a country level is obtained based on the original dataset of Milesi-Ferretti, 2024).

In the Asia-Pacific region, it has transformed from amassing foreign exchange reserves following the 1997 crisis to a calculated global investor (Basri, 2018). The proportion of debt-money assets has decreased dramatically, and FDI and equity are now important components. This has enabled the region to actively own international production capabilities and company resources. Meanwhile, its minimal dependence on derivatives proves its conservative stance. The region has been asymmetrically resilient as a stable net creditor with an average surplus of +15% of GDP. Rather than undermining its role, the global crises have transformed the Asia Pacific into a global haven and a strong source of global financial stability.

A more stable focus on investment in the real economy is observed in Africa. From 2000 to 2008, portfolio equity was particularly volatile in Africa (44.4%), but from 2016 to 2023, the share of FDIs in external assets was dominant, reaching 53.7% in 2017 and averaging 47.8%. FDI increased by 20 percentage points, the largest in the world, while equities and debt took a loss in share.

The composition of external liabilities has shifted significantly between 2000 and 2023, with a clear trend toward greater reliance on equity financing. The Americas and the Asia-Pacific region registered the biggest changes. In the Americas, for example, the share of equity portfolios increased from 15.12% to 22.62%, and debt liabilities decreased from 54.2% to 45.2%. In the Asia Pacific, FDI liabilities increased (19.6% to 26.8%) and became more central to the region's external financing structure. Europe also remained stable, with debt accounting for 55% of external liabilities as the main driver. However, unlike in other regions, Africa recorded a decrease in FDI liabilities, from 42.9% (2000–2008) to 32.8% (2016–2023), and an increase in debt, from 26.5% (2000–2008) to 32.7% (2016–2023). Portfolio equity increased from 28% to 32.6% (Fig. 3.2).

This is a more susceptible type of financial integration to the rest of the regions. The combination of a country's external liabilities—FDI, portfolio equity, debt, and financial derivatives—can determine its financial stability

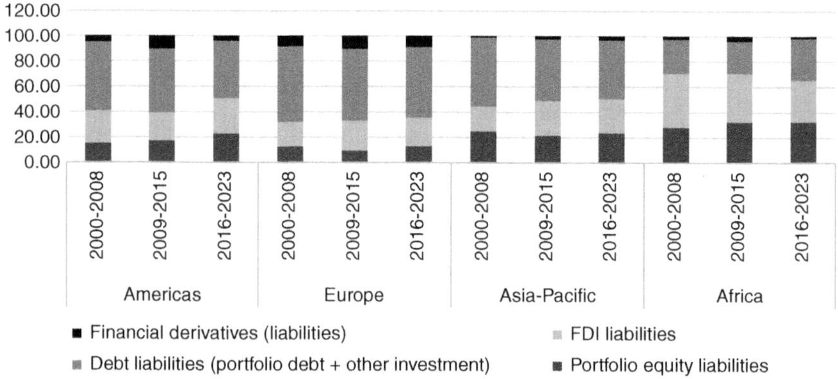


**Fig. 3.2** Change in the composition of external liabilities
Note: **The Americas** include Argentina, Brazil, Canada, Chile, Costa Rica, Mexico, and the United States.
**Europe** includes Austria, Belgium, Bulgaria, Croatia, Cyprus, the Czech Republic, Denmark, Finland, France, Germany, Greece, Hungary, Ireland, Italy, Luxembourg, Malta, the Netherlands, Norway, Poland, Portugal, Romania, Russia, the Slovak Republic, Slovenia, Spain, Sweden, Switzerland, Turkey, and the United Kingdom.
**Asia Pacific** includes Australia, China, Hong Kong, India, Japan, South Korea, New Zealand, Pakistan, and the Philippines.
**Africa** includes South Africa.
Source: Author's calculation on Milesi-Ferretti (2024) data

and is useful for understanding the structure of a country's or region's external liabilities (Ganić, 2020). The data in Fig. 3.2 demonstrate that the risk level has decreased, with a reduction in debt obligations in external financing. Debt decreased by 9 percentage points in the Americas (54.22% to 45.22% of total external liabilities composition) and in the Asia-Pacific region from 54.27% to 46.02% of total external liabilities composition.

The share of FDI liabilities increased in the Americas to 28.1% of the composition of external liabilities, the highest in the period. It stabilized at a high level in the Asia-Pacific region at 26.84%, far above the 2000–2008 average (19.62%). Europe was no exception, and the following pattern was observed: a 4-percentage-point decrease in the debt share and an unchanged FDI share, the second most significant funding source (Fig. 3.2).

The evolution of global liabilities over the past 20 years shows an interesting trend: we are increasingly turning to equity financing rather than debt financing. This indicates stronger global financial integration. For example, the United States and the Asia-Pacific region have successfully diversified, while Europe is slowly adapting to new circumstances. On the other hand, Africa is unfortunately moving in the opposite direction, increasingly relying on unstable debt financing.

## 3.3 Asymmetric Resilience and Global Financial Imbalances

Gross assets and liabilities, as shown in external balance sheets, increased rapidly in almost all countries. Those countries with high current account deficits were able to increase their gross assets thanks to high capital inflows. What is even more important is that significant changes in the structure of external balance sheets, particularly on the liabilities side, have exposed the new weaknesses (Akyüz, 2014).

External assets and liabilities are formed differently in major world regions to some extent. Over the past twenty years, the American region has faced increasing financial problems, with its debt rising from about $6.2 trillion in the early 2000s to $33 trillion in 2023 (around 120% of GDP) (Federal Reserve Bank of St. Louis, 2025). The difference between what America owes and what others owe (NIIP) has become huge. For example, the U.S. NIIP has worsened from around -22% of GDP to over -60% of GDP (U.S. Bureau of Economic Analysis, 2025). It is even harder after every crisis. The debt rose by another 11.5% of GDP during the GFC and by a further 15% during the COVID-19 crisis. It is analogous to continuing to take on new loans at usurious rates to stay afloat (Milesi-Ferretti, 2024 data).

Deep integration with structural vulnerability defines the American model of financial integration. One can explain this by noting that external balances nearly doubled, from 1.69 times GDP (2000–2005) to 3.13 times GDP (2016–2023), but with a preponderance of liabilities over assets. This leads to deterioration in net foreign assets from -20.7% of GDP to -50.4% of GDP (Table 3.1). Such a trend implies that the region is highly reliant on foreign capital, as liabilities increased faster than assets. Therefore, it must be concluded that the Americas region presents the image of a major consumer of global capital, vulnerable to shifts in

**Table 3.1** External assets (A), liabilities (L), and net foreign assets (NFA) by region

| *Region* | *Period* | *Avg_A+L (Trillion $)* | *Avg_ (A+L)/ GDP* | *Avg_ NFA/ GDP* | *Crises impact* |
|---|---|---|---|---|---|
| Americas | 2000–2005 | 23.9 | 1.69 | −0.207 | Pre-GFC impact: Moderate external buildup and manageable deficit |
| | 2006–2010 | 48.4 | 2.52 | −0.191 | During the GFC, the deficit remained stable, concealing a domestic collapse financed by foreign capital. |
| | 2011–2015 | 62.6 | 2.7 | −0.319 | Post-GFC impact: Liabilities grow faster than assets; net debt deepens. |
| | 2016–2023 | 88.1 | 3.13 | −0.504 | COVID-19 era: External balance rises sharply; NFA/GDP deficit reaches record -50%. |
| Europe | 2000–2005 | 57.2 | 4.44 | −0.067 | Pre-GFC impact: High financial integration with low net debt. |
| | 2006–2010 | 130.4 | 6.43 | −0.134 | During the GFC, integration deepens, and the NFA deficit doubles due to intra-European capital flows. |
| | 2011–2015 | 157 | 7.21 | −0.115 | Post-GFC impact: Debt crisis and rebalancing |
| | 2016–2023 | 186.1 | 8.26 | 0.038 | COVID-19 era: Europe has become a net creditor; high integration now comes with greater resilience, as confirmed during the COVID-19 pandemic. |
| Asia Pacific | 2000–2005 | 9.1 | 1.08 | 0.129 | Pre-GFC impact: Stable net creditor |
| | 2006–2010 | 19.3 | 1.44 | 0.176 | During the GFC, the crisis justifies its status as a haven, and net financial assets are rising. |
| | 2011–2015 | 30.2 | 1.48 | 0.156 | Post-GFC impact: Accumulation of external assets continues, with a large and stable surplus. |
| | 2016–2023 | 42.9 | 1.6 | 0.155 | COVID-19 era: COVID-19 resilience is one of the pillars of world financial stability. |
| Africa | 2000–2005 | 0.23 | 1.19 | −0.139 | Pre-GFC impact: Small external buildup, net debt position. |
| | 2006–2010 | 0.55 | 1.6 | −0.204 | During the GFC, vulnerability increases. |
| | 2011–2015 | 0.78 | 1.9 | −0.05 | Post-GFC impact: Recovery and improvement |
| | 2016–2023 | 0.9 | 2.51 | 0.158 | COVID-19 era: Shift to net creditors, mainly through debt reduction and commodity price impact. |

Source: Author's Milesi-Ferretti (2024) data calculation

investment mood, increases in interest rates, and currency fluctuations. The data indicate that the crises did not decelerate the external financial integration of the Americas but aggravated its quality. With a steady NFA/GDP ratio, the GFC masked the region's financial weaknesses, as foreign capital was used to cover up the internal collapse. In fact, it caused the net debt position of most countries to deteriorate due to the preponderance of liabilities over assets, as reported by Kollmann (2016) and Tang (2023). The COVID-19 pandemic has pushed the US external balance to new heights. At the same time, the net financial asset deficit has reached -50% of GDP, indicating growing vulnerability in the country's financial position, which depends on international capital flows. In contrast, the European region has maintained stable financial integration and shifted towards net lending, unlike the US.

Europa has the largest and most integrated external balance sheet, which has nearly doubled, relative to GDP, from 4.44 times GDP (2000–2005) to 8.26 times GDP (2016–2023). More importantly, Europe has recorded a historic net turnaround. Following a foreseeable negative adjustment in the GFC (-13.4% of GDP), it rebalanced to a net creditor position in 2016–2023 (+3.8% of GDP) (Table 3.1). Both qualitative and quantitative increases indicate that the high rate of integration in Europe is now supported by greater resilience.

This shift, likely spurred by the restructuring following the sovereign debt crisis, marks an irreversible transition from weak to strong incorporation into the global financial system. The data presented indicate that the Asia-Pacific region has become a net creditor, maintaining an NFA surplus of around 15–17% of the GDP.

Another interesting fact is that the region's external balance has almost quintupled, rising from $9.1 trillion to $42.9 trillion and reflecting its growing financial power. This confirms the region's capacity to serve as a sound source of capital and a strategic attraction for foreign capital. The Asia-Pacific region is an example of asymmetric resilience—global crises have not diminished its standing, but it has solidified its status as a net creditor. The countries within the region, such as China, South Korea, and Australia, dealt with the initial health and economic shock better and have recovered faster in exports. The region had been institutionalized to experience the GFC through conservative management and to hold many safe assets, a lesson learned from the 1997 Asian crisis, making it a global haven as Western economies were impacted. For example, the region demonstrated that the surplus remained stable between 2011 and 2015 (NFA/GDP: +15.6%) in the aftermath of the GFC. It continued to build external reserves during the European debt crisis and the COVID-19 crisis, keeping its surplus steady (NFA/GDP: +15.5%) and demonstrating its position as a steady capital source and a pillar of global economic stability (Table 3.1).

Africa has low volatility within a limited range, with external assets accounting for less than 1% of Europe's total. The region shifted from being a net debtor (avg NFA/GDP: -20.4% in 2006–2010) to a net creditor (avg. NFA/GDP: +15.8% in 2016–2023). However, the seemingly robust NFA of 2023 (at a historical high of $0.09 trillion) results from a 16.2% reduction in liabilities, rather than from accelerated surplus generated through asset growth (1.7% 10Y CAGR). Africa had a limited external presence and a limited deficit before the GFC of 2008, but the crisis increased its vulnerability, leading to an NFA deficit of -20.4% of GDP (Table 3.1). With the recovery of commodity prices following the crisis, the deficit shrank, and during the COVID-19 pandemic, Africa unexpectedly became a net creditor (+16% of GDP). However, this recovery is rather a result of developments on the liability side—write-offs of debts, restructuring, and less borrowing than continued accumulation of assets—and the recovery is still delicate and subject to external conditions.

Based on the above, the global financial architecture has evolved along divergent lines over the past two decades. As the Americas have become major debtors worldwide, Europe and the Asia-Pacific region have established themselves as the main creditors, albeit in different forms. Europe has adjusted after the GFC, and Asia has done so through long-term, strategic capital formation, and these two creditor centers continue to finance the growing American deficits (Milesi-Ferretti, 2023; Varoufakis, 2015).

These findings revisit the discussion on financial integration initiated by Lane and Milesi-Ferretti (2001). Ganić (2026) examines the impact of financial integration across income levels and political environments in 108 countries worldwide. The findings show that while in countries with liberalized trade and higher per capita incomes, the impact of global financial integration can be positive, in other countries, it can be neutral or negative. These results can extend the Lane and Milesi-Ferretti framework to include dynamic interactions arising from structural heterogeneity, trade openness, and integration. The key issue in the literature is whether integration has been effective. Our analysis shows that integration quality is more important than its volume is. Different integration profiles exist, unlike the typical European arc, the Asian sustainable portfolio, and the American market, all of which are based on market principles. This has prompted debates about reverting to earlier stages of integration, with a focus on progressing further and improving future integration.

## 3.4 Regional Divergence of External Positions

The world has experienced financial integration and capital liberalization over the past decades, enabling greater inflows of foreign capital, particularly in the 1990s (Akyüz, 2014). Gross foreign assets and liabilities rose in all sectors, particularly in developed nations. The value of foreign resources is approximately twice the world's GDP today or a fifth of global assets (Nievas & Sodano, 2025). Monetary policy is an important determinant of capital flows to emerging markets (Ahmed & Zlate, 2014). In fact, the authors consider interest rates to be an important determinant of net private capital inflows between emerging and developed economies.

Table 3.2 synthesizes regional market data from Milesi-Ferretti (2024). The Americas region is experiencing a worsening external sustainability crisis, and liabilities are increasing at a rate that outpaces those of any other region. For example, the net foreign assets (NFA) deficit reached a record high of $21.1 trillion in 2023.

The Americas region has experienced significant growth in its external balance sheet over the past twenty years. This primarily reflects an 8.10% annual increase in liabilities, outpacing the 7.49% growth in assets, which peaked at $64.3 trillion in 2023. This indicates that liabilities are expanding faster than assets. Consequently, NFA is in feeble health, with a -$21.1 trillion position in 2023. During the GFC, net active assets fell by 96%, while during the COVID-19 pandemic, liabilities grew faster (+ 12.8%) than assets (+10.5%), further widening the deficit by 19%. The region's increase in liabilities exceeded that in assets, indicating a tendency for net debt to rise during crises. Over the past 20 years, the Americas region has borrowed more than it has repaid, further worsening net debt, especially during recent crises. Today, the Americas are the world's largest net debtors, and their external debt continues to rise (Wilmarth, 2021).

The external balance sheet of Europe has grown at a very high rate, with assets increasing by over 8.45% annually and liabilities by 7.78%. Europe has transitioned into a net creditor, with an NFA position of $2.2 trillion in 2021, more than twice the level observed five years earlier. Both assets and liabilities in Europe experienced minimal fluctuations during the GFC and the COVID-19 pandemic, further enhancing Europe's creditor

**Table 3.2** External balance sheet dynamics by region (2000–2023)

| *Region* | *Indicators* | *Annualized growth (2000–2023)* | *Peak value $T / year* | *5Y CAGR (%)* | *10 CAGR (%)* | *GFC impact 2007/2008 vs. 2006/ 2007* | *COVID-19 impact 2020 vs. 2019* |
|---|---|---|---|---|---|---|---|
| **Americas** | Assets | 7.49% | 43.2 (2023) | 9.02% | 0.61% | -7.4% (Decline) | +10.5% (Increase) |
| | Liabilities | 8.10% | 64.3 (2023) | 6.95% | 4.27% | +2.0% (Increase) | +12.8% (Increase) |
| | NFA | – | 21.1 (2023) | 14.2% | 11.5% | Worsened by 96% | Worsened by 19% |
| **Europe** | Assets | 8.45% | 105 (2021) | 3.57% | 4.18% | -0.4% (Slight decline) | +12.7% (Increase) |
| | Liabilities | 7.78% | 102.8 (2021) | 4.06% | 5.46% | -1.7% (Decline) | +12.1% (Increase) |
| | NFA | – | 2.2 (2021) | 31% | -1.1 % | Improved by 28% | Improved Significantly |
| **Asia Pacific** | Assets | 9.15% | 26.8 (2021) | 4.66% | 4.70% | +6.0% (Increase) | +12.5% (Increase) |
| | Liabilities | 9.15% | 22.2 (2021) | 4.78% | 4.63% | -5.7% (Decline) | +15.1% (Increase) |
| | NFA | – | 4.9 (2021) | 5.35% | 4.31% | Improved by 57% | Improved by 1.0% |
| **Africa** | Assets | 7.74% | 0.55 (2017) | -3.74% | 1.04% | -4.4% (Decline) | +10.6% (Increase) |
| | Liabilities | 6.09% | 0.52 (2017) | -1.01% | -1.72% | -26.9% (Sharp decline) | -5.9% (Decrease) |
| | NFA | – | 0.09 (2021) | 18.50% | N/A | Improved by 78% | Improved by 318% |

Notes: In the case of the 10-year CAGR of net financial assets (NFA), the standard approach to calculating it cannot be used, as the values reversed sign (negative to positive) during the period under consideration. **The Americas** include Argentina, Brazil, Canada, Chile, Costa Rica, Mexico, and the United States. **Europe** includes Austria, Belgium, Bulgaria, Croatia, Cyprus, the Czech Republic, Denmark, Finland, France, Germany, Greece, Hungary, Ireland, Italy, Luxembourg, Malta, the Netherlands, Norway, Poland, Portugal, Romania, Russia, the Slovak Republic, Slovenia, Spain, Sweden, Switzerland, Turkey, and the United Kingdom. **Asia Pacific** includes Australia, China, Hong Kong, India, Japan, South Korea, New Zealand, Pakistan, and the Philippines. **Africa** includes South Africa

Source: Author's calculation on Milesi-Ferretti (2024) data

position and demonstrating its ability to manage its balance sheet in the aftermath of the European debt crisis (Hale & Juvenal, 2023).

Since 2000, the Asia-Pacific region has registered balanced annual growth of 9.15% in both external assets and liabilities. This has enabled this region to retain and enhance its net creditor position. The region's net assets have expanded by 52.4% over the past decade, reaching nearly $4.9 trillion. Assets increased by 6.0%, and liabilities decreased by 5.7% during the GFC, resulting in a 57% increase in net assets. COVID-19 has increased liabilities faster than it has increased assets. However, robust fundamentals have enabled a slight 1% increase in net assets, underscoring the region's resilience and its position as a trusted net creditor.

## 3.5 Comparative Analysis of the Impact of Crises on Global Capital Flows

Capital market integration has become integral to the globalization process (Masson, 2001). Various researchers have emphasized that global factors strongly influence capital flows (Koepke, 2019), even during periods of extreme volatility (Forbes & Warnock, 2012). The nature of the principal drivers of capital flows shifted after the GFC. Although global risk aversion used to dominate, following the GFC, global oil prices have taken over (Forbes & Warnock, 2020); exchange rates against the dollar (Erik, 2021); and US monetary policy, which had a powerful impact on bank flows, before sensitivity went back to pre-crisis trends (Avdjiev et al., 2020).

Simultaneously, whether rich or poor, each nation nowadays is a net exporter (current account surplus) and a net importer (current account deficit) of capital. Gross capital flows are typically procyclical (Broner et al., 2014). They fall apart during a crisis, as capital flows out of the country as foreign residents and domestic investors repatriate their foreign investments. A study (Rey, 2013) indicates that capital flows between regions and types of the global financial cycle are strongly correlated.

The IMF database on the world's economic prospects presents comparative estimates of the largest net exporters and importers of capital for 2000–2023 (Table 3.3). Today's acceleration of foreign investment characterizes the world economy, surpassing the rate at which world production grows. This trend has existed ever since the second half of the twentieth century. The major drivers behind such growth are the expansion of the international division of labor, internationalization of production, scientific and technological development, the close operations of transnational corporations, the opening of international trade, and the escalation of economic integration and trade (Häusler, 2002). These processes underline the growing significance of long-term investment security on a global scale.

Table 3.3 and Table 3.4 depict the flows across the various world regions and how they are now positioned at the poles of the extreme global foreign investment imbalance, with one end as the capital exporters, from -0.4% to +0.1%, and the other as the capital importers. Table 3.3 illustrates the categorization of regions worldwide as either capital exporters or importers based on their current account balances (CABs). Europe (+1.8%) and Asia Pacific (+2.3%) have permanent structural surpluses, confirming their role as net capital exporters, whereas the Americas (-2.1%) and Africa (-1.85%) remain in permanent structural deficits, identifying them as net capital importers.

Africa was the most affected by the GFC, with its CAB declining by 2.5 percentage points, whereas the Asia-Pacific region had the least impact (-0.3 percentage points). This trend was fully reversed during the COVID-19 pandemic, with Africa showing the greatest improvement (+ 1.2%) and Asia Pacific the greatest decline (-0.8%). This shift indicates a root cause of the difference in shock types. More specifically, the GFC was a financial shock that affected financially integrated regions. In contrast, COVID-19 was a real economic shock that affected regions most reliant on global supply chains.

Moreover, the findings indicate that regions with structural surpluses, such as Europe and Asia, tend to be more resilient to financial shocks. Conversely, the more volatile areas are those with deficits (Africa and the Americas). However, the COVID-19 pandemic was a different shock that struck regions with complex global production chains the hardest. The overall economic policy implication is that economic dependence on a single sector or on external financing sources should be minimized to enhance resilience to future crises (Lane & Milesi-Ferretti, 2017).

The impact of the GFC and the COVID-19 pandemic on capital flows across countries differed markedly. Countries reliant on stable foreign capital inflows were the worst affected by the GFC (UNCTAD, 2020; OECD, 2020). For the heavy capital-importing countries like Greece and Romania, the crisis was a sudden cutoff of funding. This resulted in severe recessions and fiscal tightening.

**Table 3.3** Regional capital balance during crises: GFC vs. COVID-19

| *Region/Indicator GFC* | *Average CAB* | *Change during GFC (2007–2009)* | *Change during COVID-19 (2019–2021)* | *Importer/exporter of capital* |
|---|---|---|---|---|
| America | -2.10% | -1.10 p.p. | Improvement+ 0.4 p.p. | Net importer of capital |
| Europe | 1.80% | -0.60 p.p. | Improvement + 0.5 p.p. | Net exporter of capital |
| Asia Pacific | 2.30% | -0.3 p.p. | Decline -0.80 p.p. | Net exporter of capital |
| Africa | -1.85% | -2.5 p.p. | Improvement + 1.2 p.p. | Net importer of capital |

Note: America: Argentina, Brazil, Canada, Chile, Costa Rica, Mexico, and the United States. Europe: Austria, Belgium, Bulgaria, Croatia, Cyprus, Czech Republic, Denmark, Finland, France, Germany, Greece, Hungary, Ireland, Italy, Luxembourg, Malta, the Netherlands, Norway, Poland, Portugal, Romania, Slovenia, Slovakia, Spain, Sweden, Switzerland, and the United Kingdom. Asia Pacific: Australia, China, Hong Kong, India, Japan, South Korea, New Zealand, Pakistan, and the Philippines. Africa: South Africa
Source: Author's elaboration on IMF World Economic Outlook Database

Table 3.4 presents a comparative analysis of the impacts of the GFC and the COVID-19 crises on capital-exporting and capital-importing countries. Indicatively, their current accounts temporarily improved with the decline in imports, and even Norway recorded a larger surplus owing to its energy exports.

Both Germany and the Netherlands are stable European capital exporters. Germany has also maintained a steady surplus of around 5–6% of GDP, despite both crises causing temporary declines in its CAB (from 6.7% to 5.6% during the GFC and from 7.9% to 6.9% during COVID-19). The Netherlands experienced gains from export diversification, raising its CAB from 6.8% to 10% during the pandemic. Norway is a good example of a high capital exporter, ranking among the major capital exporters with an average CAB of 13.4% of GDP.

The GFC shows that Norway achieved an impressive capital export surplus of 15.7% and has shown resilience during the COVID-19 pandemic, achieving a 14.8% recovery. On the other hand, economies in the Asia-Pacific region are quite diverse. For example, China's current account balance (CAB) has declined from 9.8% to 1.9%. This is the result of a shift from a capital export model to a consumption-led growth model

**Table 3.4** Crises' impact on major capital importers and exporters

| | *Top country exporters and importers* | *Average CAB (2000–2023)* | *GFC impact (2007–2009)* | *COVID-19 impact (2019–2021)* |
|---|---|---|---|---|
| **Strong capital exporters (> +3%)** | Norway | 13.40% | +15.7 p.p. (2008) | increase from 2.9% to 14.8% |
| | Denmark | 5.40% | from 1.5% to 3.7% | from Deficit to surplus recovery |
| | Netherlands | 6.80% | from 5.9% to 4.1% | recovery from 6.8% to 10.0% |
| | Germany | 5.60% | from 6.7% to 5.6% | Resistance (from 7.9% to 6.9%) |
| | China | 3.50% | from 9.8% to 4.7% | Stability (from 0.7% to 1.9%) |
| | South Korea | 3.20% | from 0.9% to 3.5% | Resistance (from 3.6% to 4.7%) |
| **Strong capital importers (<–3%)** | U.S. | –3.40% | Improvement (from –5.1% to –2.6%) | Deterioration (from –2.1% to –3.7%) |
| | Portugal | –4.80% | Worsening (from –9.7% to –10.3%) | Improvement (from –0.8% to –0.7%) |
| | Greece | –7.10% | Improvement (from –14.2% to –11%) | Improvement (from –1.5% to -6.3%) |
| | Romania | –5.60% | Improvement (from –13.7% to –4.7%) | Deterioration (from -4.8% to –7.2%) |
| | Spain | –3.80% | Improvement (from –9.4% to –4.0%) | Improvement (from 2.1% to 0.8%) |
| | Cyprus | –5.90% | Worsening (from -6.4% to –14.4%) | Deterioration (from –5.5% to –9.7) % |

Note: America: Argentina, Brazil, Canada, Chile, Costa Rica, Mexico, and the United States. Europe: Austria, Belgium, Bulgaria, Croatia, Cyprus, Czech Republic, Denmark, Finland, France, Germany, Greece, Hungary, Ireland, Italy, Luxembourg, Malta, the Netherlands, Norway, Poland, Portugal, Romania, Slovenia, Slovakia, Spain, Sweden, Switzerland, and the United Kingdom. Asia Pacific: Australia, China, Hong Kong, India, Japan, South Korea, New Zealand, Pakistan, and the Philippines. Africa: South Africa

Source: Author's elaboration on IMF World Economic Outlook Database (see Table 3.4). In contrast, South Korea sustained a steady average surplus of 3.20% and saw consistent recoveries during both crises, supported by its robust high-tech sector. The impact of the COVID-19 pandemic, especially in China and Germany, has reduced their surpluses relative to pre-pandemic levels (Deutsche Bundesbank, 2024).

One general implication of both global crises is that countries with diversified economies and balanced foreign policy stances toward trade have seen stable exporters or moderate capital importers show the greatest resilience. The differences in performance between Southern Europe and other peripheral economies in capital imports and exports indicate significant disparities in the structural adjustment. Portugal, Greece, and Spain, where the GFC struck a severe blow and most of which are heavy importers of capital, suffered a wretched fiscal consolidation and structural adjustment. This pushed them into a stage where they reduced their reliance on foreign capital. Remarkably, Spain even became a temporary net capital exporter (i.e., it saved more than it invested) during the pandemic, generating capital to export to others. This is a fundamental change from a chronic debt situation to a more sustainable one (Hall, 2012).

Romania and Cyprus can be seen as countries that constantly rely on foreign capital. To sustain a steady deficit, Romania requires a steady stream of capital to fund domestic investments and repair destruction. Cyprus had an even more challenging case during the pandemic, worsening its CAB from -5.5% to -9.7% of GDP. This reveals that the two economies remain structurally weak and sensitive to capital flow shocks (Lane & Milesi-Ferretti, 2017). Most countries in Southern Europe are reducing their reliance on capital imports. Romania and Cyprus saw their external positions worsen, making them more susceptible to a new financial crisis.

Asia Pacific has become a key player in global interaction over the past two decades. With its average current account surplus of 2.3% of GDP, it now operates as a net exporter of capital. It is increasingly playing a major role in international credit, while Japan and South Korea will become increasingly competitive, thanks to their high-tech assets. A key factor contributing to this boom has been the pandemic, which has increased regional connectivity and reduced daily estimates (BIS, 2023).

Europe is sending more money to other countries than it is receiving. However, there is a significant difference between the stronger economies in northern Europe and the weaker ones in southern Europe, with an average current account surplus of +1.8% of GDP. The United States is the largest net user of capital. Africa's external financial resources are highly vulnerable to fluctuations in commodity prices, making the region the most volatile. The pandemic has increased geopolitical risks and raised new concerns about global financial stability, with Europe and Asia becoming the main exporters of capital and the gap between the US and China narrowing. Meanwhile, the Asia-Pacific region is emerging as a major hub for manufacturing and finance. (Milesi-Ferretti, 2023).

## 3.6 Conclusion

Over the past two decades, the global financial debt landscape has been slowly changing. As a result of more effective debt management strategies, debt levels have been reduced by 9% in the Americas and by 8% in the Asia-Pacific region. These two world regions have reoriented themselves to attract foreign direct investment and other sources of financing.

Thanks to a slight decline in debt and a gradual increase in foreign direct investment, the European economic system remains relatively stable and balanced, though it remains vulnerable to risks. Africa, however, has taken a different course. Africa has seen a reduction in FDI (42.9% to 32.8%) and an increase in external debt (26.5% to 32.7%), reducing financial diversification.

Considering the world's tendency to reduce debt sensitivity, the rebalancing process is incoherent and unbalanced. Imbalanced resilience continues: Europe has managed to stay afloat, whereas the Americas and the Asia-Pacific region have improved their standing, and Africa is currently reacting to financial shocks.

## References

–Ahmed, S., & Zlate, A. (2014). Capital flows to emerging market economies: A brave new world? Journal of International Money and Finance, 48, 221–248. https://doi.org/10.1016/j.jimonfin.2014.05.015

–Akyüz, Y. (2014, November). Internationalization of finance and changing vulnerabilities in emerging and developing economies (UNCTAD Discussion Paper No. 217). United Nations Conference of the Disarmament and International Security. https://unctad.org/publication/internationalization-finance-and-changing-vulnerabilities-emerging-and-developing

–Avdjiev, S., Gambacorta, L., Goldberg, L. S., & Schiaffi, S. (2020). The shifting drivers of global liquidity. Journal of International Economics, 125, 103324. https://doi.org/10.1016/j.jinteco.2020.103324

–Basri, C. (2018). Twenty years after the Asian financial crisis. In L. E. Breuer, J. Guajardo, & T. Kinda (Eds.), Realizing Indonesia's economic potential (pp. 9–24). International Monetary Fund. https://doi.org/10.5089/9781484337141.071

–Bencivenga, R. V., & Smith, B. D. (1991). Financial intermediation and economic growth. Review of Economic Studies, 58(2), 195–209. https://doi.org/10.2307/2297964

–Bank for International Settlements. (2023). Inflation, external financial conditions, and macro-financial stability frameworks in Asia-Pacific: A report by a Working Group established by the Asian Consultative Council. BIS.

–Broner, F., Didier, T., Erce, A., & Schmukler, S. L. (2013). Gross capital flows: Dynamics and crises. Journal of Monetary Economics, 60(1), 113–133. https://doi.org/10.1016/j.jmoneco.2012.09.005

–Broner, F., Erce, A., Martin, A., & Ventura, J. (2014). Sovereign debt markets in turbulent times: Creditor discrimination and crowding-out effects. Journal of Monetary Economics, 61, 114–142. https://doi.org/10.1016/j.jmoneco.2013.11.004

–Caballero, J. (2021). Corporate dollar debt and depreciations: All's well that ends? Journal of Banking & Finance, 132, 106185. https://doi.org/10.1016/j.jbankfin.2021.106185

Coimbra, N., & Rey, H. (2017). *Financial cycles with heterogeneous intermediaries* (CEPR Discussion Paper No. DP11907). Centre for Economic Policy Research. https://ssrn.com/abstract=2937756

–Deutsche Bundesbank. (2024, January). Risks facing Germany arising from its economic ties with China. Monthly Report. https://www.bundesbank.de/en/publications/reports/monthly-reports/monthly-report-january-2024-773864

–Erik, F. (2021): Dominant currencies and the export supply channel, ECB Working Paper, No. 2580, ISBN 978-92-899-4802-9, European Central Bank. doi:10.2866/478644. Available at: www.ecb.europa.eu/pub/pdf/scpwps/ecb.wp2580~f3ec872727.en.pdf

–Federal Reserve Bank of St. Louis. (2025). Gross federal debt as a percentage of gross domestic product [FYGFGDQ188S]. FRED. Retrieved September 17, 2025, from https://fred.stlouisfed.org/series/FYGFGDQ188S

–Forbes, K. J., & Warnock, F. E. (2012). Capital flow waves: Surges, stops, flight, and retrenchment. Journal of International Economics, 88(2), 235–251. https://doi.org/10.1016/j.jinteco.2012.03.006

–Forbes, K. J., & Warnock, F. E. (2020). Capital flow waves—or ripples? Extreme capital flow movements since the crisis. MIT Sloan School of Management.

–Ganić, M. (2020). Financial Globalization. In: Financial Globalization in the Emerging Balkans. Palgrave Macmillan, Cham. https://doi.org/10.1007/978-3-030-65009-4_3

–Ganić, M. (2026). Financial integration and growth: Are the effects shaped by country income levels and trade liberalization? Journal of Central Banking Theory and Practice, Vol. 15, No. 2. In press.

–Gertler, M., Gilchrist, S., & Natalucci, F. M. (2007). External constraints on monetary policy and the financial accelerator. Journal of Money, Credit and Banking, 39(2–3), 295–330. https://doi.org/10.1111/j.1538-4616.2007.00019.x
–Ghironi, F., Lee, J., & Rebucci, A. (2015). The valuation channel of external adjustment. Journal of International Money and Finance, 57, 86–114. https://doi.org/10.1016/j.jimonfin.2015.03.003
–Hall, P. A. (2012). The economics and politics of the euro crisis. German Politics, 21(4), 355–371. https://doi.org/10.1080/09644008.2012.739614. Available at: https://www.tandfonline.com/doi/abs/10.1080/09644008.2012.739614
–Hale, G., & Juvenal, L. (2023). External balance sheets and the COVID-19 crisis. Journal of Banking & Finance, 147, 106570. https://doi.org/10.1016/j.jbankfin.2022.106570
–Häusler, G. (2002). The Globalization of Finance. Finance & Development, *39*(1). International Monetary Fund. https://www.imf.org/external/pubs/ft/fandd/2002/03/hausler.htm
–Imbs, J. (2004). Trade, Specialization, and Synchronization. *Review of Economics and Statistics*, *86*(3), 723–734.
–International Monetary Fund. (n.d.). World Economic Outlook Database.
–Kalemli-Ozcan, S., Manganelli, S., Papaioannou, E., & Peydró, J.-L., (2009). Financial integration and risk sharing: the role of monetary union, In: Mackowiak, B., Mongelli, F. P., Noblet, G., & Smets, F. (Eds.), *The euro at ten: lessons and challenges*, (pp. 116–155), European Central Bank.
Kalemli-Ozcan, S., Papaioannou, E., & Peydró, J. L. (2010). What lies beneath the effect of financial integration? Currency risk, legal harmonization, or trade? *Journal of International Economics*, *81*(1), 75–88. https://doi.org/10.1016/j.jinteco.2010.01.002
–Koepke, R. (2019). What drives capital flow to emerging markets? A survey of empirical literature. Journal of Economic Surveys, 33(2), 516–540. https://doi.org/10.1111/joes.12273
–Kollmann, R. (2016). International business cycles and risk sharing with uncertainty shocks and recursive preferences. Journal of Economic Dynamics and Control, 72, 115–124.
–Kose, M. A., Prasad, E. S., & Terrones, M. E. (2003). How does globalization affect the synchronization of business cycles? American Economic Review, 93(2), 57–62.
–Lane, P. R., & Milesi-Ferretti, G. M. (2001). The external wealth of nations: Measures of foreign assets and liabilities for industrial and developing countries. Journal of International Economics, 55(2), 263–294.
–Lane, P. R., & Milesi-Ferretti, G. M. (2017). *International financial integration in the aftermath of the global financial crisis* (IMF Working Paper No. 17/115). International Monetary Fund. https://doi.org/10.5089/9781484300336.001
–Lee, J. (2018). Chinese companies and the U.S. national security review. In The clash of capitalisms? Chinese companies in the United States (pp. 182–214). Cambridge University Press. https://doi.org/10.1017/9781316661802.007

– Masson, P. R. (2001). Exchange rate regime transitions, *Journal of Development Economics*, *64*(2), 571–586.

–Milesi-Ferretti, G. M. (2023). Many creditors, one large debtor: Understanding the buildup of global stock imbalances after the global financial crisis. Brookings Institution.

–Milesi-Ferretti, G. M. (2024). Missing assets: Exploring the source of data gaps in global cross-border holdings of portfolio equity. In Bank for International Settlements (Ed.), External statistics in a fragmented and uncertain world (IFC Bulletins No. 62). Bank for International Settlements.

–Nievas, G., & Sodano, A. (2025). Has the US exorbitant privilege become a rich world privilege? Rates of return and foreign assets from a global perspective, 1970–2022 (World Inequality Lab Working Paper No. 2024/14).

–Obstfeld, M., & Rogoff, K. (2009). *Global imbalances and the financial crisis: Products of common causes* (CEPR Discussion Paper No. 7606). Centre for Economic Policy Research.

–OECD. (2020, July 3). COVID-19 and global capital flows. https://www.oecd.org/coronavirus/policy-responses/covid-19-and-global-capital-flows-2f5f3c77/

–Rey, H. (2013). Dilemma, not trilemma: The global financial cycle and monetary policy independence. In Global dimensions of unconventional monetary policy (pp. 285–333). Federal Reserve Bank of Kansas City.

–Schularick, M., & Steger, T. M. (2006). Does financial integration spur economic growth? New evidence from the first era of financial globalization. Free University of Berlin.

–Tang, A. (2023). Financial integration and international dynamics: The role of volatility shocks. Mathematics, 11(23), 4742. https://www.mdpi.com/2227-7390/11/23/4742

UNCTAD. (2020). *World investment report 2020: International production beyond the pandemic* (UNCTAD/WIR/2020). United Nations.

–U.S. Bureau of Economic Analysis. (2025). International investment position. U.S. Department of Commerce. Available at: https://www.bea.gov/sites/default/files/2025-09/intinv225.pdf

–Varoufakis, Y. (2015). The global minotaur: America, Europe and the future of the world economy (3rd ed.). Zed Books.

–Wilmarth, A. E., Jr. (2021). The pandemic crisis shows that the world remains trapped in a "global doom loop" of financial instability, rising debt levels, and escalating bailouts. Banking & Financial Services Policy Report, 40(8), 1–26.

CHAPTER 4

# Basel Capital Accord and International Standard Setting

**Abstract** Chapter 4 analyzes the evolution of the Basel Capital Accord, providing a comparative review of Basel I, Basel II, and Basel III; their achievements over the years; the main areas of change; and the reasons for the upgrade to the new version. Chapter 4 also examines the level of regulatory convergence with Basel II and Basel III in 100 countries worldwide, focusing on Eastern European countries and other nonmembers of BCBS. The latest one is Basel IV, which is also briefly addressed in the last section of this chapter, devoted to the balancing of risk and financial stability. However, its worldwide acceptance is still uneven.

**Keywords** Basel Capital Accord • Banking regulation • Macroprudential regulation • Regulatory convergence • Financial stability

## 4.1 Introduction

For some time, there has been debate about whether harmonizing the supervision process is necessary. Significant turmoil in the financial world in the 1970s and 1980s was due to deteriorating bank asset quality. Many countries, mainly International Monetary Fund (IMF) members, have experienced significant banking distress. The BCBS (1988) focuses on reducing credit risk and prescribes a minimum risk-adjusted capital



M. Ganić, *Structural Change and Competitive Dynamics in Global Financial Markets*,
https://doi.org/10.1007/978-3-032-28906-3_4

ratio of 8% of risk-weighted assets (RWA). In the meantime, during the 1990s, many developing countries began transitioning to, and harmonizing, their supervisory processes and compliance with, the minimum capital threshold established under Basel I (BCBS, 1992). The transition process did not go very smoothly. The rapid financial liberalization has left many developing countries highly vulnerable to economic crises. In response to these crises, the minimum capital threshold (and other parts of the financial sector) have been unified to improve the banking regulatory environment, especially in the emerging market economies (Ganić, 2012).

Although the convergence towards Basel I has been completed, significant differences among countries worldwide remain evident. Interestingly, when the Basel Accord was launched, many lenders in developing countries did not adhere to the prescribed capital requirements, with capital adequacy ratios ranging from 2% to 5% of RWA. However, as times change, lenders have adopted new capital rules. Between 1998 and 1999, of the 103 countries covered by World Bank research (2001), only seven had a capital adequacy ratio (CAR) below 8%. On the contrary, 29 countries had a capital adequacy ratio of 10% or more, while the rest adhered to the law's prescribed capital requirements of 8%–10% of RWA.

## 4.2 Basel I

The Basel Capital Accord, also known as Basel I, is a revolutionary document that marked the first time in banking history that a single solution for capital adequacy assessment and international banking supervision was introduced. The core global banking standards were developed by the central banks of the G10 countries in the 1980s. Banking standards, known as Basel I, were originally designed to help large international banks. Their goal was to prevent unfair advantages that could arise from different regulatory rules. Although they initially focused on a small number of banks in the G10 countries, by the 1990s, more than 120 countries were planning to implement them. In fact, it had limitations at the outset; Basel I laid a solid foundation for global regulation of the banking sector (Stephanou & Mendoza, 2005).

Initially, the Basel I goal was to "strengthen the soundness and stability of the international banking system" by establishing minimum capital adequacy requirements. Also, it aims to ensure the "framework should be fair and have a high degree of consistency in its application to banks in different countries" (BCBS, 1988). Yet, Basel sets capital requirements based on each bank's assets to strengthen capital standards across the banking system. The 1999 approvals to modernize and improve Basel I, despite technical criticism, can be seen as a continuation of efforts to improve capital requirements. In fact, the BCBS proposed a minimum capital adequacy ratio of 8% of RWA, with Tier 1 capital at least 4%.

To illustrate, when a 100% risk is assigned to an unsecured loan, a bank must allocate 8% of the loan amount to capital to cover potential losses. According to Basel I, only the following weights could be assigned: 0%, 20%, 50%, and 100% risk (Fig. 4.1). The Basel capital accord treated all commercial loans equally, with a uniform capital requirement of 8% of RWA. Based on the RWA recorded in its books,

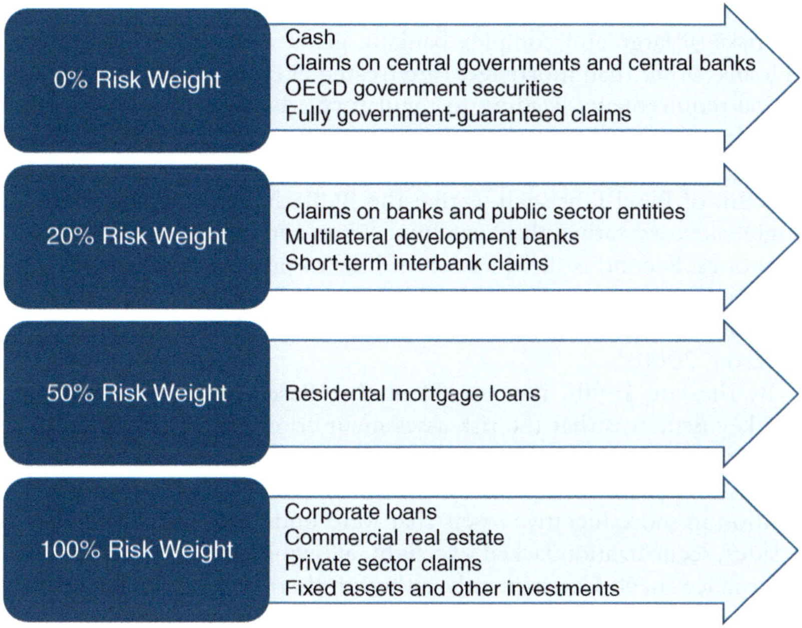


**Fig. 4.1** Risk weighting figures apply to balance sheet items
Source: *Author's compilation from* BCBS, 1988

a bank determines the required capital, which is a function of its estimated risk level. Thus, the bank's assets are differentiated by the level of estimated risk, including the conditions governing off-balance-sheet operations, which increased significantly in the 1980s. However, before that, it is necessary to determine what is meant by a capital bank in its true sense (Ganić, 2012).

Basel I divided banking capital into two classes based on their quality and function: Tier 1 (core capital) and Tier 2 (supplementary capital). Certain restrictions have been introduced, for example, limiting Tier 2's core capital to 100% of Tier 1's core capital. The bank's total regulatory capital (statutory capital level) is determined by deducting previously recorded goodwill items and investments in unconsolidated branches from core capital (BCBS, 1988).

The Basel I framework, adopted almost three decades ago, has proven very useful and productive. However, over time, it became clear that controlling large international banking groups was inadequate and too intrusive. Namely, Basel, I have shown limited risk sensitivity without providing sufficient arguments to bankers, supervisors, and the market to measure the risks of large and complex banking groups. Similarly, under Basel I, all loans (other than mortgages) are treated as equally risky and subject to capital requirements, leading to regulatory arbitrage. In other words, by changing the credit structure, banks have favored high-risk investments over low-risk ones within the same risk-weighted categories. The main criticism of Basel I, as such, is that the BCBS lumps all companies into a single category rather than grouping them into three distinct borrower categories. Second is the question of how to properly incorporate private credit ratings into its proposal. Third, Basel, I do not reduce the capital level for good credit risks or impose adequate penalties on poor credit risks (Jackson, 2000).

By the late 1990s, it was evident that Basel I had lost its objective. The key issue was that the risk assessment criteria were overly simplified, leading to regulatory arbitrage—the bank trimmed its investment in less lucrative assets deemed to carry exorbitant risk. However, it increased its position in more lucrative assets that were underestimated as being risky. Besides, securitization lacked oversight, allowing banks to shift risky assets off-balance sheet. Consequently, although there was an initial rise in capital upon the introduction of Basel I, the overall amount of capital within the banking system began to decrease; these deficiencies led to the adoption of new, more advanced standards (Lall, 2009).

## 4.3 Basel II

With developments in financial systems and banking, risk-management practices, supervisory approaches, and financial markets, Basel I was unable to keep pace (BCBS, 2001). As for any agreement, Basel I had some advantages and disadvantages. The main criticism of Basel I is that it lumps all companies into a single category rather than using three distinct borrower groupings. Second, the proper incorporation of private credit ratings into its proposal is also questioned. Third, under Basel I, clients with good credit ratings face no reduction in capital requirements, and, in some cases, they are adequately punished for having poor credit ratings. Since not all risks have been evaluated, the introduction of credit ratings into capital requirements raises the question of how to assign credit ratings to capital ratings and to credit ratings without credit ratings. Basel I have been heavily criticized for several technical and fundamental reasons. On a technical level, there has been considerable controversy over whether the BCBS was correct to incorporate private credit ratings into its document. Jackson (2000) disagrees with the Basel I rules that were formulated in 1980 and subsequently discarded in 1999. According to him, there is false and faulty reasoning in their attributing capital requirements to commercial lending, which casts a shadow on the credit rating agencies. The BCBS's initial approach to commercial loans was crude, according to Howell (2000). This was not the case in the original proposal for the Basel Capital Accord, where a distinction was made between other forms of assets (e.g., sovereign debt and bank credit). This will put all companies with different risk profiles on an equal footing when applying for commercial loans. The BCBS sought to redress this flaw by proposing to incorporate private credit ratings into CAR. Some main characteristics of Basel I and Basel II are highlighted in Fig. 4.2.

In their study, Altman and Saunders (1998) found that borrowers with the best credit ranking (AAA or AA under the Standard & Poor's system) should have a CAR of only 1.4%, while borrowers with a poor credit ranking (those ranked B and below) should have a CAR of about 17%.

Remarkably, the study also indicates substantial disparities in the respective capital expenditures of borrowers in the categories A to BBB and B to BB. However, the BCBS proposal grouped these borrowers under a single category.

The BCBS released a document titled "International Convergence of Capital Measurement and Capital Standards: A Revised Framework" on

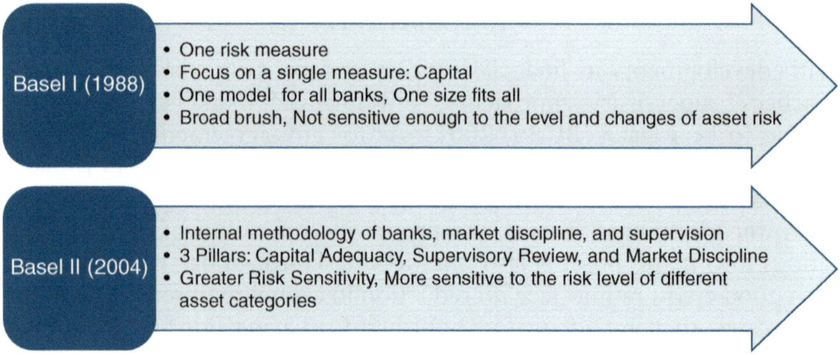


**Fig. 4.2** Basel I vs. Basel II
Source: Author's compilation on Basel Accords, BCBS (1988, 2006)

26 June 2004. This is commonly known as the Basel II accord (BCBS, 2006). As stated, Basel I incorporated credit risk and subsequent market risk. In addition, Basel II considers operational risk when determining the capital adequacy ratio alongside credit and market risk.

According to Basel II, bank regulation comprises three relevant aspects: minimum capital requirements, supervisory review by the central bank to assess the bank's adequacy, and an internal assessment process with a new emphasis on strengthening market discipline and sound banking practices (BCBS, 2006).

The purpose of the Basel II framework is to strengthen global financial stability and provide a broad overview of best practices in risk management. Ultimately, its goal is to address issues related to the stability of banks worldwide, covering three pillars: minimum capital requirements, supervisory review process, and disclosure and market discipline (BCBS, 2006).

**Pillar I: Minimum Capital Requirement**

The requirement to calculate the minimum regulatory capital builds on Basel I of 1988; nothing is new there. The new aspect of Basel II is the consideration of operational risk in CAR calculations and the inclusion of flexible approaches to RWA calculations. The calculation of the "Capital to Risk Weighted Asset Ratio" (CRAR) in Basel II and the formula are like those of Basel I. Basel II recommended at least 8% CRAR and 4% Tier One CRAR. The calculation of CRAR depends on two major determinants (BCBS, 2006):

- Eligible Total Capital Funds
- Risk-Weighted Assets

Eligible capital comprises Tier 1 (core) and Tier 2 (supplemental) capital. Compared to Tier 2 capital, Tier 1 capital is less risky and more dependable. High-risk assets: Basel II focuses on banks with stronger risk management and asset quality. The quality of assets increases, thus reducing the capital requirements, as such a pool can bear less risk.

Basel III adds additional capital, leverage, and liquidity requirements to ensure that banking institutions are not further exposed to increases in credit risk, unlike Basel I and Basel II. These regulations govern, screen, and manage risks within the banking industry.

Basel II introduced a new feature in integrated risk management that enables the determination of a bank's overall credit, trade, and operational risks. Financial costs include operational risks, and the minimum CAR must be 8% of the active risk-weighted asset. This represents a significant revision to the asset weighting method. The addition of capital requirements for operational risk, which includes losses due to process errors, internal corporate misconduct, and IT problems, is a significant innovation over Basel.

**Pillar II: Supervisory Review Process**

The first aim is to push banks to hold more capital to cover all the risks in their business, while the second aim is to develop better risk-management techniques to control and manage risks. The Pillar II has the four key aspects (BCBS, 2006):

- In line with their risk profile and capital stabilization plans, banks must assess their overall capital adequacy.
- In the area of capital management, managers must monitor the adequacy of a bank's internal capital and ensure that it complies with regulatory rules.
- Supervisors expect banks to meet minimum capital requirements and maintain their capital above a set ratio.
- Supervisors should react early to prevent negative trends and stabilize the capital adequacy ratio.

**Pillar III: Disclosure and Market Discipline**

Following the crisis, Basel II sought to rectify the shortcomings of Basel I, particularly in Pillar I, by introducing new capital and liquidity requirements. However, the probability that Basel II would entail survival following the global financial crisis was minimal. Although Basel II had created a banking structure, the GFC revealed some of its inefficiencies. This, in fact, triggered efforts to establish a new regulatory structure that would help prevent future crises. In a way, the GFC showed that Basel II had several weaknesses. Here are some key criticisms that are often heard when discussing the Basel II capital adequacy framework (BCBS, 2006):

- Minimum capital requirements for banks that failed to prevent the consequences of the global financial crisis.
- Basel II enabled banks to remove risky assets from their balance sheets through securitization, while other risks were often poorly assessed and, in some cases, underestimated.
- Basel II discouraged banks from keeping long-term assets on their balance sheets, as it was through their relocation through the OTC model (the "create and distribute" model) that the crisis began to deepen.
- The minimum capital requirements of Basel II have proven to be procyclical, especially with the deepening of the crisis, when loan losses have become more frequent and can threaten the bank's solvency. This procyclicality has diminished a bank's ability to make loans, worsening liquidity in the financial market.

Basel II had significant shortcomings in its capital buffers, as large banks used the A-IRB method to reduce their capital reserves by more than 40%. In contrast, smaller banks, relying on the standardized approach, faced higher capital requirements. This reduced the profits of smaller banks and increased their risk of acquisition. The regulation favored large, systemically important banks, creating competitive hurdles for smaller institutions and exposing structural issues in Basel II's design.

Based on empirical analysis, this resulted from structural bias in the policymaking process, in which the tremendous lobbying by multinational banks tilted the standards toward more advanced methods that favored their business models. Regional banks from developing and emerging markets, such as India and South Africa, argued during the consultation that implementing A-IRB could create competitive asymmetries and enable regulatory arbitrage benefiting large megabanks. However, their objections were raised retrospectively and not given due attention, leading to the enactment of laws that legalized the inequality. This case illustrates how powerful financial institutions can influence international standards for small firms and economic stability (Lall, 2009).

Furthermore, the most significant criticism of Basel II is that it contributed to the GFC. In particular, the BCBS acknowledged the defects in the countercyclical effects of minimum capital requirements. To address these deficiencies, the Basel Committee developed additional measures, including allocating additional provisions for expected credit losses on exposures and increasing the countercyclical capital buffer (BCBS, 2009).

## 4.4 Basel III

Basel III was established as a direct response to the financial crisis of 2007–2008. Moreover, it was adopted at the end of 2010. Basel III builds on the guidelines of the Basel II agreement, which led to significant deficiencies in banks' ability to manage risks, particularly in their liquidity and capital (Ganić, 2012). Its focus is on the stability of individual banks rather than on relationships within the banking system. The microprudential regulations are intended to make institutions more transparent and stable but have inadvertently added to the fragility of the risk system, as noted by the Warwick Commission (2009). Basel III attempted to ease this strain by incorporating more detailed regulations connecting microprudential and macroprudential procedures. This two-pronged approach serves to increase the stability of the financial sector against external shocks and the spread of crises, reducing the risks associated with specific organizations and contagion mechanisms across all systems (The Warwick Commission, 2011). Basel III was developed to increase transparency and improve banks' response to shocks arising from governance and financial issues. Among the changes introduced in Basel II and Basel III was the idea that regulators should abandon the established rules-based rules used to approve capital expenditures and instead implement principles-based rules (BCBS, 2011).

The GFC has highlighted numerous problems with the structure, amount, and quality of banks' capital. Likewise, the GFC has shown that meeting minimum capital requirements for banks does not necessarily ensure the stability of the banking sector. After the dramatic collapse of Lehman Brothers, politicians, banking regulators and national policymakers met to address the problem of "too big to fail" institutions and how to make banking more secure and more valuable to all parties, in September of 2010, a group of governors of the leading countries and

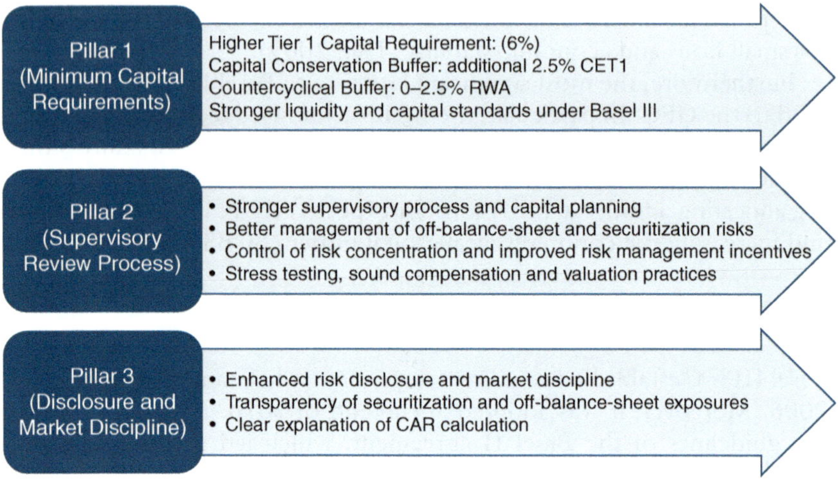


**Fig. 4.3** Basel II vs. Basel III
Source: Author's compilation on Basel II and Basel III, BCBS (2006, 2011)

national regulators, in the presence of the representatives of the BCBS, announce agreement after two days talks, paving the way for strengthening the existing capital framework (BCBS, 2010) The main elements of global financial reform were formally announced in November of 2010 in Seoul at the G20 Leaders' Summit. They include the introduction of global minimum liquidity standards and changes to risk-based capital requirements. The proposed Basel II reform package changed the foundations of Basel II, raised capital standards globally, and established standards for capital reserve creation.

Together with the measures to improve Basel II standards (from July 2009), the announced proposals represent a comprehensive response by the Committee to the impact of the GFC on regulation, supervision, and the management of banking risks. The key elements of the Basel III regulation are that it raises the quality and consistency of the capital base and strengthens the risk coverage of the capital framework (Walter, 2011). This is a primary objective of the reform.

The primary elements are as follows: The proposals are structured around the following regulatory objectives: increased quality and quantity of capital; reduced leverage by introducing a backstop leverage ratio;

increased liquidity coverage; and strengthened risk capture, notably counterparty risk (BCBS, 2011).

In recent years, Basel's standards have undergone significant changes, including improvements and a shift from Basel II to Basel III, as summarized in Fig. 4.3. The Basel III package proposes a new common equity requirement of 4.5% of a bank's RWA. Under the proposal, this applies to the current 2% RWA in common shares, including a capital conservation buffer of 2.5% of common shares. This ultimately suggests that a practical requirement of 7% for common shares would be appropriate. If the capital falls within a "buffer zone" between 4.5% and 7%, the bank faces restrictions on dividend and employee bonus payments. Including a capital conservation buffer of 2.5% protects banks against adverse effects during financial disturbances (Cecchetti, 2010). According to Basel II, additional capital allocations in buffer zones were not prescribed. These reforms, innovations, and extensions progressively and significantly increased capital requirements, while the cost of capital will be monitored closely.

The key characteristics of Basel III are as follows (BCBS, 2011):

The bank has enhanced the quality, consolidation, and transparency of its core capital. The new rules do not have some of the elements that used to fall in Tier 1. Their primary role is to enhance the capacity of individual banks and increase their capital. Other components of the capital structure are also coordinated by the board in the process of enhancing the quality of Common Equity Tier 1.

Both paid-in capital and retained earnings, along with the funds required to compute Tier 2 capital, are included under the heart of Common Equity Tier 1.

To control liquidity risk, Basel III introduced two new liquidity ratios. The first one refers to the minimum global liquidity risk for internationally active banks and consists of a 30-day monthly liquidity ratio. The second refers to the long-term (structural) liquidity ratio.

Basel III includes key methods for identifying and assessing liquidity risk trends at the level of individual banks and the entire banking sector. The rules and regulations are consistent with the principles of liquidity management and control developed by the BCBS in September 2008.

Furthermore, banking institutions are required to have sufficient liquid assets to cope with market difficulties (a monthly liquidity ratio has been developed) and invest in regular, high-quality assets that can be sold quickly if necessary.

The liquidity coverage ratio (LCR) and the net stable funding ratio (NSFR) are designed to monitor and maintain liquidity. For example, the LCR requires banks to maintain cash and other liquid assets, while the NSFR requires banks to hold more long-term funding (BCBS, 2013).

Another challenge banks face, arising from reforms, innovations, and extensions from Basel II to Basel III, is the liquidity risk ratio requirement. Banks face the challenge of integrating their current risk and finance systems to address this risk.

However, to ensure concentration of funding, banks will be required to maintain a continuous hierarchical account of the agreed counterparties.

Banks must produce different liquidity coverage ratios for each consolidation level and currency in accordance with credit risk rules. Internationally operating banks must manage in accordance with national discretion and local regulatory standards, while aligning them with the new liquidity ratio rules.

The idea of introducing a countercyclical buffer is to protect the buffer zone, enabling banks to preserve capital to offset losses from financial and economic downturns. The equity buffer zone is between 0% and 2.5% of RWA and comprises common shares and other capital components that can absorb losses. Regulations are tailored to each country's specific context (Griffith-Jones et al., 2011).

## 4.5 Basel II and Basel III Adoption: A Cross-Regional Comparison

This section examines convergence with international banking standards and evaluates the progress in implementing Basel II and Basel III worldwide in recent years. To analyze this aspect, survey data from FSI (2015) are used to examine the extent and speed of adoption of Basel II and Basel III in fewer than 100 countries that were not part of BSBC. Specifically, the study uses 10 Basel II and 8 Basel III subcomponents from 2004 to 2015 to examine whether all 18 subcomponents were introduced across all 101 countries.

The main objective of the FSI survey was to explore ongoing changes in the convergence process from Basel II to Basel III for jurisdictions selected by the BCBS. According to the World Bank classification, these jurisdictions are divided into five groups: East and West Asia (14 countries),

Europe and Central Asia (28 countries), Latin America and the Caribbean (23 countries), Middle East and North Africa (12 countries), Sub-Saharan Africa (19 countries), and South Asia (5 countries).

Although Basel II has significant variations in implementation at the national and regional levels, its widespread adoption is noted in several jurisdictions not covered by the BCBS, according to the FSI questionnaire.

By 2015, for example, in East Asia and the Pacific, of the 14 surveyed countries, only 3 countries had adopted any Basel II components, while Chinese Taipei was the only country to implement all Basel II subcomponents. Moreover, in the MENA region, all 12 surveyed countries implemented at least one Basel II element. In Europe and Central Asia, we found that Serbia, Norway, Liechtenstein, and Iceland fully comply with Basel II and have adopted all 10 subcomponents. At the same time, the Kyrgyz Republic and Moldova made no progress in implementing Basel II. Similar findings exist in other jurisdictions, such as South Asia, which includes Laos and Bhutan. By contrast, Bangladesh, Nepal, and Pakistan have each adopted at least one aspect of Basel II.

Meanwhile, in some regions, such as Sub-Saharan Africa, 11 countries have not taken any measures to implement Basel II. In Latin America and the Caribbean, 13 countries have not taken steps.

As shown in Fig. 4.4, the highest percentage of Basel II adoption is in Europe and Central Asia (52%), followed by East Asia and the Pacific (39%), the Middle East and North Africa (38%), and South Asia (28%). The lowest levels of adoption were in Latin America and the Caribbean (10%) and Sub-Saharan Africa (13.5%).

On the contrary, very low convergence with Basel III is observed among many non-implementers in surveyed countries. As you can see, the highest rate of adoption of Basle III is found in the Middle East and North Africa (25%), followed by South Asia (22.5%), Europe and Central Asia (18%), East Asia and Pacific (17%), Sub-Saharan Africa (12.5%), and Latin America and the Caribbean with only 4.5% adoption.

The data in Figs. 4.5 and 4.6 reveal that many surveyed jurisdictions still have regulatory convergence structures inadequate for the Basel II and Basel III standards. Moreover, based on the FSI (2015) survey data about the level of regular convergence with Basel II, we found that:

Most of the surveyed countries adopted requirements for credit risk (SA: Standardized approach) and operational risk (BIA: Basic indicator approach) in the current implementation of Pillar 1, Pillar 2, and Pillar 3,

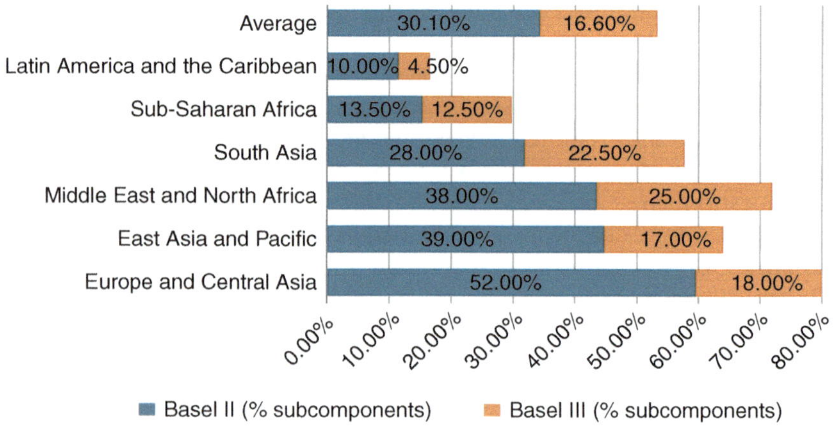


**Fig. 4.4** Cross-regional variation in implementation of Basel II and Basel III
Note: Europe and Central Asia - 28 countries, East Asia and Pacific - 14 countries, Latin America and the Caribbean - 23 countries, Middle East and North Africa - 12 countries, Sub-Saharan Africa - 19 countries, and South Asia - 5 countries.
Source: Authors' elaboration on FIS (2015) survey data

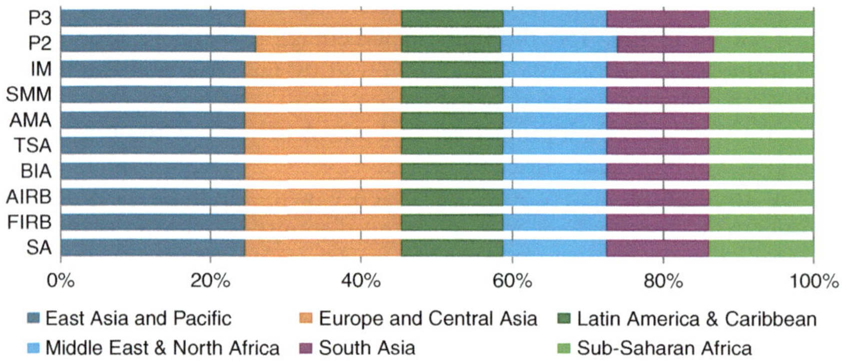


**Fig. 4.5** Implementation of key components of Basel II
Note: Basel II: Pillar 1 - credit risk: SA = standardized approach, FIRB = foundation internal ratings-based approach, A-IRB = advanced internal ratings-based approach; Pillar 1 - operational risk: BIA = basic indicator approach, TSA = standardized/alternative standardized approach, AMA = advanced measurement approaches; Pillar 1 - market risk: SMM = standardized measurement method, IM = internal models; P2 = Pillar 2; P3 = Pillar 3
Source: Authors' elaboration on FIS (2015) survey data

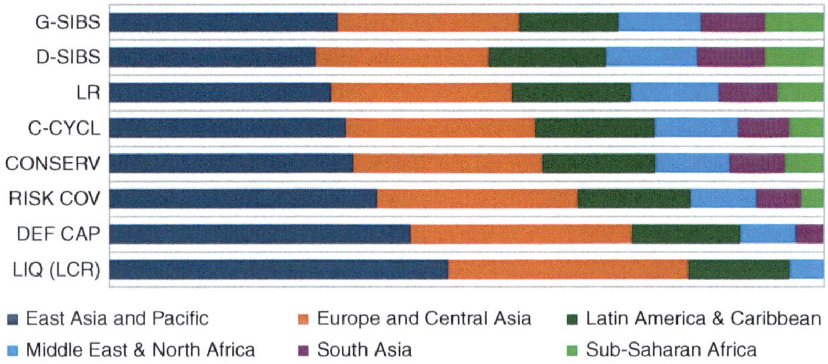


**Fig. 4.6** Implementation of key components of Basel III
Note: Basel III: Liq = liquidity standard; Def cap = definition of capital; Risk cov = risk coverage; Conserv = capital conservation buffer; C-cycl = countercyclical capital buffer; LR = leverage ratio
Source: Authors' elaboration on FIS (2015) survey data

with the highest percentage of adoption in Europe, Central Asia, and the Middle East and North Africa regions.

Pillar 1, Pillar 2, and Pillar 3 of Basel II show very low convergence across most surveyed jurisdictions, such as the Caribbean, Sub-Saharan Africa, and Latin America, with implementation rates of 15% or lower. Figure 4.5 shows regional differences in the implementation of Basel II standards outside the BCBS and the EU. East Asia and the Pacific (18.2%) and Europe and Central Asia (15.0%) have higher implementation rates, especially for Pillar 2, due to stronger financial integration and regulatory capacity.

Regions such as Latin America and the Caribbean, the Middle East and North Africa, Sub-Saharan Africa, and South Asia implemented only about 10% of Basel II components. This indicates that Basel II implementation remains fragmented, with more advanced regions adopting more Basel II components, while most areas meet only the minimum requirements.

On the other side, Basel III enforcement was weak across all regions (Fig. 4.6).

The highest adoption rates of Basel III components were observed in East Asia and the Pacific (15.1%) and Europe and Central Asia (11.8%). In comparison, Latin America and the Caribbean (6.9%), South Asia (3.4%), and Sub-Saharan Africa (2.5%) recorded the lowest levels of Basel III implementation.

These findings support the claim of regulatory convergence with some exceptions (Lall, 2009). Although the Basel Framework is assumed to be implemented equally across regions, our cross-regional measurements for Basel III indicate persistent disparities. This shows that regulatory arbitrage persists in the global system and that the drive towards global standards is a genuine expression of national will.

## 4.6 Strengthening Resilience: Basel IV Risk-Sensitive Reforms

The Basel III reforms package, also referred to as Basel IV in its final stage, presents the next step in the transformation of global banking standards. The framework aims to strengthen the quality of risk assessment on credit products, operations, and activities and enhance capital allocation principles to avoid future bank failures. Despite the reform's introduction in 2017, it has never been fully embraced, even in a large economy like the United States. The proposed rules will be decided on by regulators in January 2024, during which they will take time to listen to stakeholders in a public consultation. This is a slow process, and it shows how difficult it is to align intervention regulations across nations. Though it is not an easy task to implement, all of this can fit within the main idea of Basel IV: strengthening the banking sector through more accurate risk assessment and prudential requirements.

The new regulations require banks to perform dynamic loan reclassification based on borrowers' risk profiles—such as reevaluating loans to growing businesses—and to adjust risk weights accordingly. Basel IV refers to the final stage of Basel III reforms, comprising two main packages that cover specific regulatory areas (Schneider et al., 2017).

The first package contains major reforms designed to improve risk management and financial stability, as follows (Feridun & Özün, 2020):

*FRTB (Fundamental Review of the Trading Book): Improves market risk standards.*

*Counterparty Credit Risk: The risk involved in providing credit exposure to third parties.*

*NSFR (Net Stable Funding Ratio): Establishes a long-term liquidity standard to ensure stable funding even under stress.*

*Leverage Ratio*: Restrains excessive lending by requiring the minimum capital-to-exposure ratio.
*Considerable Exposure*: Caps expose clients to concentration risk.
*Market Risk*: Brings new, better tools for managing price-fluctuation risks.

The second package emphasizes credit, market, and operational risk frameworks (BCBS, 2017a):

*Credit Risk*: Changes in the Standardized Approach SA-CR and tighter measures for internal credit risk models.
*Credit Risk Mitigation*: New tools for helping to minimize possible losses.
*Market Risk*: Greater advances in the practices concerned with risk assessment.
*Operational Risk*: New capital requirements based on real losses in the past.
*Output Floors*: A minimum threshold with a minimum requirement of risk-weighted assets not being lower than 72.5% of those used under the standardized approach.
*Sustainability*: Long-term measures for the stability of the banking sector.
*Credit valuation adjustment (CVA) risk*: New standards for treating valuation adjustments arising from changes in the market.

Under Basel IV, there are significant reforms to address flaws in earlier standards, particularly the over-reliance on internal risk models. Key changes include the following (BCBS, 2017a):

- Tighter restrictions on internal model use.
- Internal models are prohibited for some portfolios (e.g., large firms with a turnover exceeding €500 million).
- The capital floor on the IRB approach increases the capital requirement.
- New capital charges—for overdrafts and unconditionally cancellable loans.
- Increased risk weights on subordinated debt and commercial real estate.
- Stricter collateral and guarantee rules.

- Diminished ability to shift assets between banking and trading books
- The general goal is consistency and transparency and to restore banks' trust in regulators.
- Central Regulatory Changes in Basel IV:
  - Internal Models (IRB).
  - Use of IRB models is now restricted.
  - Not allowed for large corporations with a turnover exceeding €500 million.
  - The capital floor is established at 72.5% of the standardized approach.
  - Reduced use of Advanced IRB (A-IRB), especially for real estate.

Real Estate Exposure:

- New methodologies introduced
- The standard operating method now relies on the Loan-to-Value (LTV) ratio.
- Stricter rules on collateral eligibility
- Capital Requirements:

### 4.6.1 EU Response to Basel IV: Regulatory Changes, ESG Change, and Transition Measures

The idea of reforming Basel III was followed by efforts to develop a new proposal, commonly referred to as Basel IV. This is a comprehensive package that aims to (1) improve approaches to measuring credit and operational risk exposures; (2) revise the credit valuation adjustment (CVA) approach; (3) set up an output floor that limits the reduction of capital requirements; (4) update the leverage ratio framework with detailed requirements relating to global systemically important banks (G-SIBs); and (5) integrate revised market risk standards that were first consulted on in January 2016. (Feridun and Özün, 2020).

Reforming Basel III, commonly referred to as Basel IV, was planned to start on January 1, 2022, with a gradual implementation of the floor for the IRB approach's input parameters and to finish on January 1, 2027. However, the implementation was postponed by 12 months because of the COVID-19 pandemic, with full implementation now set for January 1, 2028.

The Basel III reforms could have significantly affected the banking sector in the EU. This new EU legislation established the Capital Requirements Regulation (CRR3) and the Capital Requirements Directive (CRD6) to apply Basel IV across all EU banks, not just those operating internationally. One notable point is the proposal to cut capital requirements for low-risk residential mortgages under internal ratings-based (IRB) methods—a clear contrast to the calibration of Basel IV, which is more stringent. The adoption of the Basel III reform as part of the EU banking package (CRR3 and CRD6) was initially scheduled to begin at the start of 2023. However, it was delayed until the beginning of 2025 due to the COVID-19 pandemic, and its implementation will proceed gradually until 2032 (EBA, 2024a).

Within the package of reforms, which go a step further than what was proposed in Basel III, there are several important measures. First, there are temporary capital requirements that will apply to exposure to crypto assets. Next, we have the integration of ESG risks into prudential frameworks, which includes mandatory disclosures, improved risk-management procedures, and enhanced supervision. Finally, there is a reformed regulatory framework that applies to non-EU bank branches that are established in the EU.

The new framework mandates that banks regularly report on ESG risks, including their identification, measurement, and management (CRR3 Article 87a).

The CRD6 limits banks' cross-border operations by establishing firewalls through strict selection processes, management standards, and reorganization requirements. Significant implementation dates will involve ESG risk standards, which will be in place in January 2026, and third-country company rules, which will be in place in January 2027. Transitional arrangements are also guided by CRR3, specifically a gradual 10 percent credit conversion factor for unconditionally canceled liabilities and the removal of the basis and eligibility criteria for companies to be rated (EBA, 2024b).

The EU applies the IRB approach input floor on three bases: individual bank, consolidated, and sub-consolidated. Under the standardized approach to unrated corporate exposures, the risk weight is 100%. To increase comparability between standardized and internal models and to improve the reliability of RWA, the framework applies new input floors to banks that use internal models. These floors limit capital calculations under the Standardized Approach, making it more closely aligned with the risk-sensitivity objectives of Basel IV.

## 4.7 Conclusion

From a general perspective, the Basel Capital Accord represented incremental reforms in setting global banking standards, starting with Basel I and extending to Basel II and Basel III. It can affect every bank to varying degrees, depending on type, size, and location. Once fully implemented, Basel III guidelines will increase capital buffers and require strict recovery costs for key risks, liquidity, and credit. Adding centralized credit lines and reducing the coverage of rating agencies are other goals of the Basel III strategy. The goal is to improve the financial system. Basel III introduced standards and guidelines to close the gaps identified in Basel II. With rapidly evolving global markets, these regulations might need to be revised and standards expanded over time as the accords are put to work to develop into a different set of rules to respond to the changes demanded by the markets.

Now, senior management and board members are increasingly aware of stricter regulations and greater accountability for risk management as financial innovation continues to emerge. Reforming Basel III, commonly referred to as Basel IV, has the potential to transform international banking standards by addressing sensitivity to systemic risk, capital buffers, and financial stability. In any case, it has not been entirely successful, and the minimal improvement underscores the need to align various regulatory systems. These priorities of global uniformity and the domestic economy contradict the European Commission's model, which incorporates production for the covered period and the capital's local tasks.

As regulators increasingly focus on risk management, reforming Basel III, commonly referred to as Basel IV, strengthens risk management, increases capital buffers, and enhances financial stability, raising banking standards in financial innovation. However, due to the complexity of ensuring compatibility across multiple regulatory systems, even large organizations, such as the EU, do not always successfully implement these standards. The EU uses a tailored approach with short-term pauses and specific capital requirements, highlighting the conflict between national economic goals and global stability. The goal is to strike a balance between national standards and local markets, enabling financial systems to develop and survive.

## References

–Altman, E. I., & Saunders, A. (1998). Credit risk measurement: Developments over the last 20 years. Journal of Banking & Finance, 21(11–12), 1721–1742. https://doi.org/10.1016/S0378-4266(97)00036-8

–Basel Committee on Banking Supervision. (1988). *International convergence of capital measurement and capital standards*. Bank for International Settlements. http://www.bis.org/publ/bcbs04a.pdf

–Basel Committee on Banking Supervision (BCBS). (1992). Report on International Developments in Banking Supervision. Basel: Bank for International Settlements.

–Basel Committee on Banking Supervision (BCBS). (2001). Compendium of documents produced by the Basel Committee on Banking Supervision (Vols. 1-3). Bank for International Settlements. Available at: https://www.bis.org/publ/bcbsc001.htm

–Basel Committee on Banking Supervision (BCBS). (2006). International Convergence of Capital Measurement and Capital Standards, Bank for International Settlements. Available from: http://www.bis.org/publ/bcbs128.pdf

–Basel Committee on Banking Supervision (BCBS). (2009). Range of Practices and issues in Economic Capital Frameworks, Bank for International Settlements. Available from: < http://www.bis.org/publ/bcbs152.pdf

–Basel Committee on Banking Supervision. (2010). *Basel III: A global regulatory framework for more resilient banks and banking systems*. Bank for International Settlements. https://www.bis.org/publ/bcbs189.htm

–Basel Committee on Banking Supervision (BCBS). (2011). Basel III: A global regulatory framework for more resilient banks and banking systems, Bank for International Settlements. Available from: http://www.bis.org/publ/bcbs189.pdf http://www.bis.org/publ/bcbs238.pdf, http://www.bis.org/publ/bcbs282.pdf [2nd June 2014].

–Bank for International Settlements (BCBS). (2017a), Basel III: Finalising Post-crisis Reforms, December 2017, available at: https://www.bis.org/bcbs/publ/d424.pdf

–Bank for International Settlements (BCBS). (2017b), High-level Summary of Basel III Reforms, December 2017, available at: https://www.bis.org/bcbs/publ/d424_hlsummary.pdf

–Cecchetti, S. G. (2010). Financial reform: a progress report, National Institute of Economic and Social Research, London, 4 October (2010).

–European Banking Authority (EBA). (2024a). Final Draft Implementing Technical Standards amending Commission Implementing Regulation (EU) 2021/451 on supervisory reporting referred to in Article 430 (7) of Regulation (EU) No 575/2013 concerning output floor, credit risk, market risk, operational risk, crypto assets and leverage ratio. EBA-ITS/2024/06. Available at: https://www.eba.europa.eu/sites/default/files/2024-07/b6be4507-e772-4bfb-a8f4-631f424ed12a/final_report_on_amendments_to_the_its_on_supervisory_reporting-crr3_crd6.pdf

–European Banking Authority (EBA). (2024b). EBA FINAL SINGLE PROGRAMMING DOCUMENT 2024–2026. Available at: https://www.eba.europa.eu/sites/default/files/2024-01/a9b1c021-821b-4718-9a9b-2691bba32cc3/EBA%202024-2026%20SPD%20FINAL.pdf

–Feridun, M. & Özün, A. (2020). Basel IV implementation: a review of the case of the European Union", Feridun, M. & Özün, A. (2020). Basel IV implementation: a review of the case of the European Union", Journal of Capital Markets Studies, Vol. 4 No. 1, pp. 7–24. https://doi.org/10.1108/JCMS-04-2020-0006
–Financial Stability Institute. (2015). *FSI survey on Basel II, 2.5 and III implementation* (FSI Papers No. 6). Bank for International Settlements. https://www.bis.org/fsi/fsiop2015.htm
–Ganić, M. (2012). Međunarodna regulacija u bankarstvu, International University of Sarajevo, First issue, Sarajevo.
–Griffith-Jones, S., Spiegel, S., & Thiemann, M. (2011). Recent Development in Regulation in the Light of the Global Financial Crisis: Implications for Developing Countries: Background note prepared for the IPD, UN DESA, Ford Foundation and FEPS Inter-Regional Workshop "Managing the Capital Account and Regulating the Financial Sector- A Developing Countries Perspective" in Rio de Janeiro on the 23rd and 24th of August 2011.: Initiative for Policy Dialogue, Columbia University.
–Howell, E. J. (2000). The Role of Credit Rating Agencies in the Establishment of Capital Standards for Financial Institutions in a Global Economy. SSRN Electronic Journal DOI:10.2139/ssrn.250166.
–Jackson, P. (2001). *Bank capital standards: The new Basel Accord. Bank of England Quarterly Bulletin*, Spring 2001, 1–8. https://ssrn.com/abstract=759528
–Lall, R. (2009). Why Basel II Failed and Why Any Basel III is Doomed. Oxford: Global Economic Governance Programme.
–Schneider, S., Schröck, G., Koch, S., & Schneider, R. (2017). Basel "IV": What is next for banks? Implications of intermediate results of new regulatory rules for European banks. McKinsey Global Risk Practice. Available at: https://www.mckinsey.com/~/media/mckinsey/businessfunctions/risk/our%20insights/basel%20iv%20whats%20next%20for%20banks/basel-iv-whats-next-for-banks.pd
–Stephanou, C., & Mendoza, J.C. (2005). Credit risk measurement under Basel II: An overview and implementation issues for developing countries. In the World Bank Policy Research Working Paper. Washington, DC: World Bank. SSRN. https://ssrn.com/abstract=708342
–The Warwick Commission. (2009). *In Praise of Unlevel Playing Fields*. Warwick: University of Warwick.
–The Warwick Commission. (2011). The Warwick Commission on International Financial Reform: In Praise of Unlevel Playing Fields. Warwick: University of Warwick.
–Walter, S. (2011). *Basel III: Stronger banks and a more resilient financial system* [Conference presentation]. Conference on Basel III, Financial Stability Institute, Basel, Switzerland. https://www.bis.org/speeches/sp110406.pdf
–World Bank. (2001). Comments on the Basel Committee's New Capital Framework' and covering letter, June, on www.bis.org

CHAPTER 5

# The Global Foreign Exchange Market: Structure, Evolution, and Currency Dynamics

**Abstract** This chapter examines the development of the foreign exchange market (Forex) and analyzes trends across major financial centers worldwide. This research is descriptive and quantitative, based on detailed data from the BIS central banks' surveys conducted from 2001 to 2022. It examines global trends in exchange rates, currency pairs, and trading instruments, including their regional distribution. To identify important trends, such as the growing influence of currency swaps and the rise of the Chinese yuan, the analysis also uses CAGR calculations and market share analysis. After that, comparative regional analysis shows different development paths across world regions.

**Keywords** Foreign exchange market (FOREX) • OTC FX turnover • Currency dynamics • Currency pairs • Geographical distribution of FX trading



M. Ganić, *Structural Change and Competitive Dynamics in Global Financial Markets*,
https://doi.org/10.1007/978-3-032-28906-3_5

## 5.1 Introduction

Exporting companies need to decide whether to maintain their currency exposure or speculate on currency movements during periods of fluctuation. As a result, derivative markets—such as forwards, futures, options, and swaps—have developed to both reduce risks and generate returns. This highlights the importance of accurate exchange rate prediction.

According to Rahmadani (2025), supply and demand in the foreign exchange market will grow again. Both descriptive and quantitative methods are used to study long-term trends. The main source of information is a series of questionnaires conducted by the Bank for International Settlements (BIS) over a three-year period (2001–2022), which allows for a unique assessment of international retail foreign exchange trading.

Exchange rates, financial instruments, and their regional distribution over 21 years were determined using this data collection. The calculation includes compound annual growth rate (CAGR) to identify key trends. Interest rate forecasts and market share costs are also included in the analysis to predict the outcome. During this period, the growing importance of currency swaps and the rapid rise of the Chinese Yuan (CNY) became evident. Not surprisingly, these phenomena are of key importance to study.

## 5.2 Declines and Changes in FX Turnover

The FX market is essential to a country's financial system, serving as a key connector and reflecting the growing integration of the national economy with the global one. Its main functions are to facilitate international payments and maintain the country's international liquidity. The FX market is a global network of buyers and sellers of foreign currency, and it is neither centralized nor strictly controlled by any institution or country. Also, the FX market is the most liquid financial market in the world, with daily turnover exceeding $5 trillion and more than 10 times that of the global equity market (Cespa et al., 2022). It is a convincingly significant segment of the financial market, with a marked continuity of growth driven by the development of international trade and economic activity. This applies particularly to China and India, as well as to the countries of the former Soviet Union, which have begun to play an increasingly important role in world trade.

One of the most exciting aspects of the currency market is that in 2022, it traded over $7.5 billion per day (BIS, 2022). These transglobal trade

**Table 5.1** Currency shares in OTC FX turnover (2001–2022)

| *Currency* | *2001 Share* | *2022 Share* | *Δ (2001–2022)* | *Key observations* |
|---|---|---|---|---|
| USD | 89.86% | 88.45% | −1.41 p.p. | 2013–2016 recovery (+1.5 p.p.) |
| EUR | 37.91% | 30.54% | −7.37 p.p. | 2010 peak (39.04%) |
| JPY | 23.53% | 16.70% | −6.83 p.p. | 2013 rebound (23.05%) |
| GBP | 13.05% | 12.90% | −0.15 p.p. | Stable despite Brexit |
| CNY | 0.01% | 7.01% | +7.00 p.p. | 2016–2022 surge (+3.02 p.p.) |
| AUD | 4.32% | 6.38% | +2.06 p.p. | 2013 peak (8.64%) |
| CAD | 4.49% | 6.21% | +1.72 p.p. | 2022 15-year high |
| CHF | 5.98% | 5.19% | −0.79 p.p. | 2007 peak (6.82%) |
| HKD | 2.24% | 2.58% | +0.34 p.p. | 2019 peak (3.54%) |
| SGD | 1.05% | 2.43% | +1.38 p.p. | Steady ASEAN growth |

Note: USD - United States Dollar, EUR - Euro, JPY - Japan Yen, GBP - Great Britain Pound, CAD - Canadian Dollar, AUD - Australia Dollar, CHF - Swiss Franc, CNY - Chinese Yuan, HKD - Hong Kong Dollar, SGD - Singapore Dollar (Net basis, percentage shares of average daily turnover in April)
Source: Author's elaboration on BIS (2022) data, Triennial Central Bank Survey Foreign exchange turnover in April 2022

streams have, over the last 20 years, returned money into the limelight. Table 5.1 presents data on traded currencies from the BIS survey (2022), which covered 53 central banks and almost 1,300 financial institutions. The 2001–2022 environment of the global FX market shows striking consistency and significant shifts in currency dominance.

For example, USD reshares increased from 84.9% to 89.9%. Although it dipped to 84.86% in 2010, growth picked up again by 2022, reaching 88.45%, reaffirming its role as the primary international reserve and trading currency.

The euro's highest level was observed in 2010, when it stood at 39.04%, and dropped to 30.54% (2022), mainly because of Brexit and reduced volatility of EUR/USD (Table 5.1). CNY has seen impressive growth, with its share rising from 0.01% in 2001 to 7.01% in 2022, a 700-fold increase. This increase, fueled by the emergence of offshore CNH markets (Hong Kong and London); the trade arrangements included in the Belt and Road Initiative; and its inclusion in the IMF SDR basket (with the weight of 10.9%), has enabled it to replace the Australian and Canadian dollars as the fifth most traded currency in the world.

On the other hand, the Japanese yen (JPY) experienced the largest decline among major currencies, falling from 23.53% to 16.70%. The main reason for this decline was the decreased attractiveness of carry-trade yield opportunities relative to their value. Meanwhile, despite the Brexit controversy, the price remains stable. Notably, the pound accounted for 12.90% in 2022, slightly less than its 13.05% share in 2001.

Traditional currencies like the Japanese yen were still falling (from 23.53% to 16.7%), whereas resource-linked currencies such as the AUD and CAD exhibit cyclical changes. Therefore, AUD's share of trade in OTC foreign exchange instruments was 8.64% (2013), and CAD's share was 6.21% (2022), reflecting a difference in the trajectory of the commodity market (Table 5.1).

Among smaller currencies, the Singapore dollar (SGD) has doubled twice (1% to 2.4%) because financial integration in Asia has proved successful, and the Swiss franc's safe-haven status has kept it at around 5%.

The FX market is a global, decentralized financial market that is technologically well-equipped and where banks, corporations, governments, and institutional investors trade currencies. Banks facilitate investment and trading activities for their corporate and institutional clients and are ready to offer or exchange a wide range of currencies. Traditionally, money flows between currencies and is dependent on import and export transactions. Speculative trading in currencies began to take precedence in the FX market, especially after 1973, following the collapse of the Bretton Woods system, when exchange rates among major currencies became floating (Chen, 2012). Most national currencies operate under a floating exchange rate regime, in which exchange rates fluctuate daily in response to market forces. The free interaction between demand and supply of foreign currency in the FX market determines exchange rates. As with all prices, foreign exchange rates can be expressed in two ways. First, how many units of the local currency are needed to buy a unit of foreign currency (direct quotation)? Second, how many units of the foreign currency can be obtained for one unit of the domestic currency (indirect quotations–represented in the UK)?

As Table 5.2 demonstrates, there are significant variations in the share of the currency pair in OTC FX turnover. It is important to note that most trading in the FX market is in USD against other currencies. As an illustration, USD/EUR, USD/JPY, and USD/GBP are the most traded currency pairs in the global FX market, accounting for more than 50% of total turnover.

**Table 5.2** Comparative trends OTC FX turnover by leading currency pair (2001 vs. 2022)

| *Currency pair* | *2001 share* | *2022 share* | △ **Share** | *Turnover growth* | *Turnover in $B 2022* | *Peak* |
|---|---|---|---|---|---|---|
| USD/EUR | 30% | 22.79% | −7.3 p.p. | 4.6x | 1,706 | 2001 peak (30%) |
| USD/JPY | 20% | 13.50% | −6.5 p.p. | 4.1x | 1,014 | 2001 peak (20%) |
| USD/GBP | 10% | 9.50% | −0.5 p.p. | 5.76x | 714 | 2004 peak (13%) |
| USD/CNY | - | 6.60% | +6.6 p.p. | 495x (since 2004)* | 495 | 2022 peak (6.6%) |
| USD/CAD | 4% | 5.50% | +1.5 p.p. | 8.2x | 410 | 2022 peak (5.5%) |

*A growth of 495x is calculated since 2004, when FX turnover was first recorded (0.1–0.2).
Note: Because two currencies were involved in each transaction, the sum of the percentage shares of the individual currencies totals 200% rather than 100% (Net basis, daily averages in billions of USD and percentages)
Source: Author's elaboration on BIS (2022) data

The development of global FX turnover has shown persistent trends and dramatic shifts in the dominance of currency pairs over the last 20 years.

The USD/EUR currency pair was the most traded, but its market share declined from 30% in 2001 to 22.7% in 2022, even as the total daily absolute turnover grew from $372 billion to $1.7 trillion. The decline in FX market share suggests that the euro's share in global finance diminished, although it remains the primary alternative to the USD (Table 5.2).

During this period, the share of the USD/JPY exchange rate fell from 20% (2001) to 13.5% (2022). The decline reflects Japan's prolonged low-yield environment or low-interest-rate policy. The USD/GBP exchange rate remains relatively stable, with the pound maintaining a share of 9–10% until Brexit-related turbulence. The rise of the USD/CNY exchange rate to fourth place (accounting for 6.6% or $495 billion) highlights a gradual shift in the global influence of currencies, with particular emphasis on the geopolitical dimensions of capital redistribution. Namely, the increasing use of the yuan in international trade symbolizes this shift.

With a 5.5% share, the USD/CAD exchange rate remained relatively stable in 2022. (Table 5.2) The massive growth of currency pairs in recent years has transformed trade around the world. Based on BIS data, the rise of the USD/CNY exchange rate to fourth place signals the geopolitical significance of ongoing capital flow redistribution.

## 5.3 Dynamism of the Global OTC FX Market

The instruments that are used in the foreign exchange market have varied over the past few decades. This has been because of changes in regulatory and risk-management techniques. Table 5.3 presents over-the-counter (OTC) foreign exchange (FX) trading, by instrument type, around the world, 2001–22. This is the data provided by the BIS trading analysis. Brokers demonstrate three trends. These are the further prevalence of currency swaps, the structural deterioration of spot trading, and the rise in future contracts due to the pandemic.

FX swaps remain the dominant one, with a 50.8% share and a steady medium-term outlook, projected to grow at a 21-year compound annual growth rate (CAGR) of 8.7%. Nevertheless, outright forwards have increased significantly, resulting in the highest growth with a 6.5% CAGR over five years, almost double their long-term average of 10.1%, led by corporate hedging needs during COVID-19.

In fact, there is a structural decline in FX spot transactions. During this period, their share of turnover fell from approximately 31% to 28%. On the other hand, their annualized growth rate (2013–2022) decreased by 0.3%, reflecting lower spot trading volumes (Table 5.3).

Over the past two decades, currency swaps have experienced the highest growth rate, with a 21-year CAGR of 10.82%. Despite this, they account for only about 1.7% of total OTC FX turnover. FX options, on the other

**Table 5.3** OTC FX turnover by instrument (in billions of USD)

| *Instrument* | *Average turnover ($B)* | *Annualized growth (2016–2022)* | *Annualized growth (2013–2022)* | *21Y CAGR (2001–2022)* |
|---|---|---|---|---|
| FX Swaps | 2346.75 | 8.2% | 5.4% | 8.73% |
| Spot Transactions | 1412.38 | 4.1% | 0.3% | 8.44% |
| Outright Forwards | 551 | 6.5% | 4.4% | 10.08% |
| Currency Swaps | 59.5 | 5.9% | 6.1% | 10.82% |
| FX Options | 199.75 | 3% | 1.3% | 9.22% |

Note: The BIS Triennial Survey questions for the years 2001, 2004, 2007, 2010, 2013, 2016, 2019, and 2022 are used to calculate the CAGR. Geometric growth rates are used for periods that do not coincide with the survey periods (e.g., 2016–2022)

Source: Author's elaboration on BIS (2022) data. BIS, Triennial Survey of foreign exchange and OTC derivatives trading, 2001–2022 hand, have stagnated, with annualized growth rates of 1.3% (2013–2022) and 3% (2016–2022). These trends became even more evident during the COVID-19 pandemic from 2019 to 2022. Forwards and swaps recorded higher growth rates than options, despite market conditions that usually support options trading (Table 5.3).

As a result of the GFC, spot market trading increased approximately 48% in 2010 compared to 2007 (BIS, 2010; Reserve Bank of Australia, 2010). Basel III regulations had some implications for derivative markets, particularly for swaps and forward transactions. COVID-19 has also increased the frequency of forward trading (see Table 5.3). According to the BIS Triennial Survey (2022) data, we found that the trend of expanding forward trading activity continues, especially evident from 2019 to 2022.

To facilitate comparison of turnover in the OTC market worldwide, the countries under study have been grouped into four central regions: America, Europe, Asia Pacific, and Africa. Table 5.4 shows specific patterns in the geographical expansion of the OTC FX market from 1992 to 2025.

The OTC FX market experienced significant changes in its geographic distribution between 1992 and 2025. Combined, the European and American markets account for over 70% of global OTC foreign exchange turnover. It contributes to the overall market stability. In the European market, the largest OTC FX market saw a turnover of $5.8 trillion in 2025, while the second-largest OTC FX market is America, with a turnover of $2.6 trillion in 2025.

The Asia-Pacific market is one of the fastest-growing regions and is projected to reach over $3.4 trillion by 2025, surpassing the Americas and becoming a key market worldwide. It is registering high growth in both developed and emerging countries, with a compound annual growth rate (CAGR) of 7.6%, close to the CAGR of the Americas (7.9%) and Europe (7.7%). The African region has experienced a steady expansion with a CAGR of 5.7% despite significant volatility. Between 2019 and 2022, the region experienced a downturn, followed by consistent growth through 2025 (Table 5.4).

An examination of how the crisis affected the geographical distribution of the OTC FX market reveals that regions exhibited heterogeneous sensitivity to global economic shocks. The GFC led to a minor decrease in turnover in the Americas and Europe in 2010 relative to 2007. However, both had recovered comparatively quickly with the support of expansionary monetary policies. The RBI (2012) confirms that governments and central banks have employed unconventional policy measures

**Table 5.4** Geographical distribution of OTC FX by regions (in billions of USD)

| *Region* | *1992* | *2025* | *Growth (1992–2025 in $B)* | *CAGR (1992–2025)* | *Peak (year)* | *The impact of crises* |
|---|---|---|---|---|---|---|
| America | 203.9 | 2,645.1 | +2,441.2 | +7.9% | 2019 | Slight decline in 2008/09, recovery by 2025 |
| Europe | 513.3 | 5,806.6 | +5,293.3 | +7.7% | 2025 | Decline in 2016, recovery by 2025 |
| Asia Pacific | 296.7 | 3,431.4 | +3,134.7 | +7.6% | 2025 | Stable growth, except for a slight decline in 2010. |
| Africa | 3.4 | 21.4 | +18.0 | +5.7% | 2025 | Oscillations, decline 2019–2022, recovery 2025 |

Note: **America region:** Argentina, Brazil, Canada, Chile, Colombia, the United States, and Mexico. **Asia-Pacific region:** Australia, China, Hong Kong SAR, India, Japan, South Korea, New Zealand, the Philippines, and Singapore. **Europe region:** Austria, Belgium, Bulgaria, Cyprus, the Czech Republic, Denmark, Estonia, Finland, France, Germany, Greece, Hungary, Ireland, Italy, Luxembourg, the Netherlands, Poland, Portugal, Romania, Slovenia, the Slovak Republic, Spain, and the UK

Source: Author's elaboration on BIS (2025b) data. BIS, Triennial Survey of foreign exchange and OTC derivatives trading, 1992–2025

to correct the situation over the last two years. It is worth noting that such approaches focus on short-term comparisons between financial markets and the economy. According to Ebury (2020), the consequences of the pandemic are dire, and the Federal Reserve System (Fed) has repeatedly loosened its monetary policy since the start of the crisis. To counter the effect of the financial crash of 2008/09, the central bank has reduced its main policy rate by 100 basis points to an effective lower bound (0–0.25%). Also, the Fed reintroduced its quantitative easing (QE) program, initially described as a $700 billion asset purchase program. However, the Fed has since pledged to purchase unlimited amounts of U.S. Treasury and mortgage-backed securities (Ebury, 2020).

The Eurozone crisis (2011–2012) further damaged the European market, which declined in 2013 and again in 2016 before stabilizing and continuing to grow in 2019. However, the COVID-19 pandemic caused temporary disruptions across regions. The Americas, Europe, and the Asia-Pacific region grew, but Africa experienced a decline in FX market activity from 2019 to 2022 due to lower liquidity and weakened integration into global financial flows. However, during the most recent period, 2022–2025, all regions are showing renewed growth, with Asia Pacific and the Americas leading, indicating that the market has consolidated and that confidence lost during the years of disruption is gradually restored (Table 5.4).

In the context of the OTC FX market's geographic dispersion, Europe is the unquestionable worldwide leader, with a turnover still larger than that of the Americas and the Asia-Pacific region (BIS, 2025a).

Due to the long-standing economic problems and structural shifts in global markets, the Americas region is lagging behind Asia despite continued growth. With a share decreasing by only 1%, Africa remains a marginal market participant. However, it shows steady growth and significant potential for further expansion, especially with improved financial infrastructure and stronger links to global economies. Despite this progress, market concentration remains very high, with three regions (Europe, Asia Pacific, and the Americas) accounting for more than 99% of global OTC foreign exchange turnover. This indicates little geographical diversification and dominance by the world's leading financial centers.

## 5.4 The Impact of Crises on the Geographic Structure of the OTC FX Market

The geographical developments observed in the OTC FX trading process over the last three years have demonstrated varying regional trends in growth, stability during crises, and growth prospects. Table 5.5 provides a regional analysis of the development of the OTC FX market between 1992 and 2025, showing key indicators: total turnover, market shares, average annual growth, and growth during various crises.

According to data, the European market is worth $5.8 trillion by 2025, accounting for 49.2% of the global market (BIS, 2025a). Europe maintained its leading position despite the eurozone being severely affected by the crisis, which led to a 11.7% decline from 2013 to 2016 (Baba & Packer, 2009; Melvin & Taylor, 2009). During the COVID-19 pandemic, the United States recorded a -2.2% decline and remained the second-largest global market, with a share of 22.2% by 2025 (BIS, 2025a). The Asia-Pacific region has become the fastest-growing region. Growth was 17.5% during the GFC, 21.4% during the European financial crisis, and 3.7% during the COVID-19 pandemic. In 2025, the region reached a market level of 28.8%.

**Table 5.5** Regional development of the OTC FX market: Key indicators

| *Region* | *Share 2025* | *Growth 1992–2025 (x times)* | *CAGR 1992–2025* | *Impact of GFC (07–10)* | *Impact of Euro crisis (13–16)* | *Impact of COVID-19 (19–22)* |
|---|---|---|---|---|---|---|
| Europe | 49.2% | 11.3x | 7.7% | +20.7% | −11.7% | +6.4% |
| America | 22.4% | 13.0x | 7.9% | +20.3% | +1.2% | −2.2% |
| Asia Pacific | 29.1% | 11.6x | 7.6% | +17.5% | +21.4% | +3.7% |
| Africa | 0.2% | 6.3x | 5.7% | +2.9% | +1.4% | −22.2% |
| Total | 100% | 11.7x | 7.6% | +19.7% | +2.7% | +2.6% |

Source: Author's elaboration on BIS (2025b) data. BIS, Triennial Survey of foreign exchange and OTC derivatives trading

It might also be confirmed by similar research by Eichengreen & Kawai (2015) and McCauley (2018) on the euro crises and by BIS (2025a) on the COVID-19 pandemic.

Although Africa is registering a decent long-term growth rate of 5.7%, it remains a marginal market, accounting for 0.2% of total turnover. It has been the most susceptible to the pandemic, experiencing a 22.5% drop (Table 5.5).

Overall, global OTC FX turnover has increased 11.7-fold between 1992 and 2025, with an average growth rate of 7.6%, though crises have had varied effects across regions. The Asia-Pacific region was more resilient, America experienced mixed performances, and Europe was more vulnerable during the eurozone crisis. Africa was the most severely affected by the pandemic (Table 5.5). Furthermore, Table 5.6 details the concentration and growth dynamics of the OTC FX market in 2025 for the ten largest countries.

Indicators included in this data cover global long-term trends, growth dynamics since 1992, and the impact of the COVID-19 pandemic. The top ten countries account for 94.9% of the global market, amounting to $11.18 trillion (2025), while the remaining countries together account for 5.1%. This shows a high level of market concentration in the global OTC FX market.

The United Kingdom remains in the lead with a turnover of $4.74 trillion, representing 42.4% of the global OTC FX market, and has seen 16-fold growth since 1992 at an average annual rate of 8.9%. The second-largest OTC FX market is the United States, with a share of 20.9% and turnover of $2.3 trillion. This represents a 12.9-fold increase, though

**Table 5.6** Top 10 countries in the OTC FX market (2025): Concentration and growth

| *Rank* | *Country* | *Turnover 2025 (billion USD)* | *Share in 2025* | *Turnover 1992 (billion USD)* | *Growth 1992–2025 (x times)* | *CAGR 1992–2025* | *Change 2019–2022 (COVID-19)* |
|---|---|---|---|---|---|---|---|
| 1 | U.K | 4,742.6 | 42.4% | 297.2 | 16.0x | 8.9% | +5% |
| 2 | U.S. | 2,334.7 | 20.9% | 181.6 | 12.9x | 7.9% | +39.6% |
| 3 | Singapore | 1,485.3 | 13.3% | 75.9 | 19.6x | 9.5% | +45.3% |
| 4 | Hong Kong | 883.1 | 7.9% | 60.9 | 14.5x | 8.5% | +9.9% |
| 5 | Japan | 440.2 | 3.9% | 126.1 | 3.5x | 3.9% | +12.2% |
| 6 | Germany | 386.1 | 3.5% | 56.5 | 6.8x | 5.85% | +102.4% |
| 7 | France | 242.2 | 2.2% | 35.3 | 6.9x | 5.86% | +44.9% |
| 8 | Canada | 232.7 | 2.1% | 22.3 | 10.4x | 7.4% | +20% |
| 9 | China | 235.1 | 2.1% | 0.0 | intensive growth | >20% | +12.3% |
| 10 | Australia | 200.9 | 1.8% | 29.6 | 6.8x | 6.0% | 0% |
| Σ | Top 10 | 11,182.9 | 100% | 885.4 | 12.6x | 8.0% | +18.3% |
| The rest of the countries | 721.6 | 5.1% | 131.9 | 5.5x | 5.2% | 507.5 | |

Note: Baseline year before the pandemic (2019); Peak of the pandemic (2022)
Source: Author's elaboration on BIS (2025b) data. BIS, Triennial Survey of foreign exchange and OTC derivatives trading

still below the UK's 16-fold expansion. The Asian financial centers have recorded particularly sharp growth in the OTC FX market. For example, Singapore is third worldwide with a share of 13.3% and the largest rise among the top countries, at 19.6-fold; Hong Kong registered a 14.5-fold increase.

In 2025, China accounted for 2.1% of the total, with a turnover of $235 billion. Between 2019 and 2022, growth rates in developed countries increased notably. For instance, Canada experienced a 57.6% increase, Germany a 102.4% increase, Singapore a 45.3% increase, France a 44.9% increase, and the U.S. a 39.6% increase. In contrast, the United Kingdom experienced a modest 5% increase during the same period (see Table 5.6).

Interestingly, the top ten countries have experienced an average long-term growth rate of 8% between 1992 and 2025, higher than the cross-country average (5.2%) for the remaining countries. This indicates an increasing level of market concentration and a shift of global FX activity toward major financial centers at the expense of smaller markets.

## 5.5 Conclusion

The structure of the international FX market was radically revamped, and this can be condensed into three core tendencies. To begin with, the current dominance of the United States dollar and its key role in global finance and in dollar-denominated financial markets. Second, there is a gradual shift in financial activity to the East, replacing the classic Western centers with Asian-Pacific ones (Singapore, Tokyo, and Hong Kong), including the increasing integration of China into global finance. Third, the unprecedented rise of derivatives as risk-creation tools in FX activity.

While London and New York remain at the forefront of the global financial world, cities such as Singapore, Hong Kong, and Tokyo are increasingly growing and strengthening their position, joining China in the global financial system. Europe continues to hold a dominant position amid challenges such as the eurozone crisis, while the Americas and the Asia-Pacific region are showing resilience and growth through crises such as COVID-19. At the global level, trade turnover is highly concentrated: 10 countries account for 95% of global turnover, led by the UK, the US, and major Asian financial centers such as Singapore and Hong Kong.

## References

–Baba, N., & Packer, F. (2009). From turmoil to crisis: Dislocations in the FX swap market before and after the failure of Lehman Brothers (BIS Working Paper No. 285). Bank for International Settlements.

–Bank for International Settlements. (2010). Triennial Central Bank Survey of Foreign Exchange and OTC Derivatives Market Activity in April 2010 - Preliminary Global Results - Turnover. Bank for International Settlements.

–Bank for International Settlements. (2025a). Triennial Central Bank Survey: Foreign exchange turnover in April 2025. Bank for International Settlements. https://www.bis.org/statistics/rpfx25.htm

–Bank for International Settlements. (2025b) data. BIS, Triennial Survey of foreign exchange and OTC derivatives trading. https://www.bis.org/statistics/rpfx25_ir.htm

–Cespa, G., Gargano, A., Riddiough, S. J., & Sarno, L. (2022). Foreign exchange volume. *Review of Financial Studies*, *35*(5), 2386–2427. https://doi.org/10.1093/rfs/hhab095
–Chen, J. (2012). Essentials of Foreign Exchange Trading John Wiley & Sons, 9 Mar 2009 Retrieved 2012-07-13 ISBN 0470390867
–Bank for International Settlements. (2022). Triennial Central Bank Survey: Foreign exchange turnover in April 2022. Bank for International Settlements. https://www.bis.org/statistics/rpfx22.htm
–Ebury. (2020). G3 FX Update: the impact of Covid-19 so far and short-term expectations*. Ebury Partners. (Internal market report, no longer publicly available).
–Eichengreen, B., & Kawai, M. (2015). Renminbi internationalization: Achievements, prospects, and challenges. Brookings Institution Press.
–McCauley, R.N. (2018). The 2008 crisis and the international monetary system (BIS Papers No. 100). Bank for International Settlements.
–Melvin, M., & Taylor, M.P. (2009). The global financial crisis: Causes, threats and opportunities. Journal of International Money and Finance, 28(8), 1243–1262.
–Reserve Bank of India. (2012). Reports: Financial Markets. Reserve Bank of India. https://rbi.org.in/scripts/PublicationReportDetails.aspx?ID=669.
–Reserve Bank of Australia. (2010). Activity in global foreign exchange markets. RBA Bulletin, December 2010. https://www.rba.gov.au/publications/bulletin/2010/dec/pdf/bu-1210-6.pdf.

CHAPTER 6

# The Reshaping of Global Corporate Finance: From West to East

**Abstract** The chapter centers on a major change in corporate debt worldwide. It maps the emerging geography of corporate debt, characterized by a twofold change. The first is an increase in the issuance of international bonds, and the second is a shift in market power from the West to the East. The US and Europe now share the stage with the Asia-Pacific region, whose rapid growth has changed the global center of gravity. The new landscape offers greater access to capital but is inherently more complex, characterized by regional segregation, fragmentation in Europe, and high volatility in emerging markets.

**Keywords** Debt market expansion • Corporate debt financing • Crisis impact (GFC/COVID-19) • Decoupling • Market volatility analysis

## 6.1 Introduction

A bond is a contract detailing the terms of the debt. It determines when the issuer will settle its principal liabilities and the date to which interest will be paid, based on the use of investor funds. The interest rate paid



M. Ganić, *Structural Change and Competitive Dynamics in Global Financial Markets*,
https://doi.org/10.1007/978-3-032-28906-3_6

on a bond is called the coupon. Bonds are debt securities that are sold by corporations, governments, and other governmental organizations to finance their daily commitments and to finance capital projects, including schools, hospitals, highways, or infrastructure. Bond buyers are investors who provide the issuer with funds in exchange for interest payments, with the principal repaid to them at maturity. Unlike stocks, bonds are interest-bearing securities that investors can purchase directly from the issuer (Fabozzi, 2002).

Unlike ordinary shares, which have a permanent life, the bonds have a limited lifespan. The period during which the issuer has promised to fulfill the terms of obligations is called maturity. Before the 1970s, the stereotypes were real, but the bond market has evolved tremendously since then (Pilbeam, 2010). There are types of bonds issued that do not promise a fixed income. In contrast, others are associated with a significant number of risks. The common denominator of most bonds is that they are debt securities that give the holder defined rights to receive interest over the life of the bond and to recover the principal without conferring ownership or management rights in the issuer (Choudhry, 2006).

## 6.2 Bond Market Innovations

A bond market is part of the financial system and plays an important role in firms' financing. Over the past 30 years, many financial innovations have emerged in the bond market. These innovations have been developed to benefit both issuers and investors and to reduce potential risks.

Accordingly, several such financial innovations in bond markets are presented here and explained: convertible bonds, bonds with call and put options, bonds with variable interest rates, callable bonds, industrial development bonds (IDBs), liquid yield option notes, joint bonds, guaranteed bonds, inverse floaters, catastrophe bonds (CAT), and indexed bonds.

**Bonds with call and put options**: For bonds with a call option, the issuer can withdraw the bonds before maturity if funding costs fall, thereby returning money to investors. The reason for activating the call option is that it is profitable for the issuer to issue new bonds at a lower interest rate, thereby reducing financing costs (Neftci & Santos, 2003).

**Put bonds:** These can be sold back to the issuer at a specified period before maturity. With a put option, the investor does not have to wait for the statute of limitations to expire and can repay the debt at any time.

When interest rates rise, investors can use a put option because it is physically possible to convert their new capital into higher-yielding stocks.

**Convertible bonds:** These are bonds issued with an option to replace them, giving the owner the right to exchange them for other securities, i.e., to convert them into other property, for a specified future period. Convertible bonds are usually converted into the company's ordinary or preference shares, although they can sometimes be converted into variable-rate notes (Connolly, 1998; Stowell, 2018).

**Eurobonds:** These are bonds issued outside the country of issuance. For example, bonds issued in USD in London or in yen in New York are considered eurobonds. These bonds can be straight with a fixed interest rate or involve ongoing bond purchases, among other variations. While governments issue Eurobonds, corporations do so more frequently.

**Bonds with variable interest rate:** These are corporate bonds with variable-rate coupons indexed to a short-term interest rate. They can be set at predetermined intervals. This type of bond protects the bondholder from rising inflation. These bonds generate interest payments tied to the current market interest rate. The interest rate on these bonds is variable and adjusts with market movements. The most common adjustment is to bind to a reference rate, such as LIBOR (Levinson, 2010). A coupon is determined every six months upon payment.

**Callable bond:** According to the US Securities and Exchange Commission (2014), callable or redeemable bonds are bonds that the issuer may redeem before maturity. On the call date, the issuer has the right, but not the obligation, to abandon the bond and pay the call price to the bondholder. It is the bond's nominal value plus the accumulated interest up to that point (Levinson, 2010).

The main cause of the call is the decline in interest rates. As market interest rates decrease, issuers seek to refinance their debt at a lower cost, resulting in the calling of already-issued bonds and the issuance of new bonds at lower interest rates.

Typically, the interest rate (or coupon) on callable bonds is higher than that on non-callable bonds because investors face greater risk and the issuer has the option to call the bond (Chen, Mao & Wang, 2010).

There are three primary types of call features, including the following (SEC, 2014):

- **Optional Redemption.** The issuer has the right, not the obligation, to redeem the bonds. Many municipal bonds feature optional

call provisions that issuers may exercise after a certain period, often 10 years.
- **Sinking Fund Redemption** requires the issuer to regularly set aside funds to pay off the bonds before their maturity.
- **Extraordinary Redemption** allows the issuer to call back its bonds before maturity if specific events occur, such as damage or destruction of the project financed by the bonds.

**Industrial development bonds (IDBs):** Industrial development bonds are a type of income tax-exempt bond. They issue bonds to support private business initiatives, such as building or purchasing a factory or acquiring heavy machinery or equipment. The government aims to improve the economy and labor demand in each region through these financial instruments. The main advantage of these bonds is that they allow private companies to borrow money at a lower-than-market interest rate.

The interest rate on IDBs is typically 2–4 percentage points lower than taxable alternatives.

The local community where the entity is situated usually benefits economically from the positive effect on the local tax base resulting from job creation and/or job retention associated with the expansion project.

**LYON (Liquid Yield Option Note):** LYON was introduced by Merrill Lynch in 1985. It refers to convertible zero-coupon bonds that are callable by the issuer and putable by the investor. None of these four features of LYONs (zero-coupon, convertible, callable, and putable) was new, but their combination makes LYONs innovative in bond markets. LYON is issued at a large discount on the par value, as it does not pay interest. It is usually offered by corporations with broad name recognition but volatile equity (McConnel & Schwartz, 1986).

**Guaranteed bonds:** Guaranteed bonds are bonds in which a third party, such as a bank, insurance company, another corporation, or government authority (as with municipal bonds), guarantees payment of interest and principal. It aims to reduce default risk by guaranteeing that a third party will pay the investor interest and principal in the event of the issuing company's insolvency or bankruptcy. In exchange for guaranteeing, the third party receives fees from the issuing company. Because of lowered risk, these bonds usually offer lower interest rates. Guaranteed bonds benefit both issuers and guarantors, as issuers have access to debt financing at a lower cost (due to lower interest rates).

In contrast, guarantors receive a fee for incurring the risk. Guaranteed corporate bonds, which comprised approximately 14% of all corporate bonds issued in the United States between 1993 and 2012, have remained a sought-after area. With this form of guarantee, also known as a credit enhancement, the bond guarantor will pay investors if the issuer fails to make payments (Chen, Huang, Sun & Yu, 2020).

**Catastrophe bonds (CAT)**: The catastrophe in the 1990s taught the insurance companies a good lesson—they needed to transfer the risk to all security holders in capital markets (Litzenberger, Beaglehole, and Reynolds, 1996). One such instrument was developed in 1994. This instrument is the cat bond. This instrument aims to increase funding and provide sufficient resources in the event of a catastrophe. Other organizations, such as pension funds, are the most common buyers of such bonds. Investors are motivated to invest in this type of security if insurance companies offer favorable, attractive interest rates. These securities can be designed to experience single or multiple losses. Catastrophe bonds are high-yield bonds designed to raise funds in the event of a specified catastrophe (e.g., a hurricane or earthquake). The special condition states that if the issuer incurs a loss resulting from a predefined catastrophe, the payment of interest and principal will be deferred or fully forgiven. The advantage for investors is that they can obtain a higher yield for almost the same level of risk. Cat bonds could not be used as the sole security to hedge risk; therefore, risk swaps entered the hybrid securities market. Risk swaps function the same way cat bonds do, with the only difference being that the party issuing the risk swap takes an equal amount of risk of an adverse event happening as the cat bond does (Stuart & Kari, 2002).

**Inflation-indexed bonds:** These are corporate bonds whose coupon can be adjusted for changes in inflation and is linked to a specific price index, often the Consumer Price Index. While other bonds have a maturity date (redemption value) fixed in nominal terms and, due to inflation, may suffer a decline in real value, this type of bond is attractive to risk-averse investors seeking to monetize their expectations about a stock index's movement. This type of bond is valuable to investors because its real value is known at the time of purchase, eliminating uncertainty-related risk and making it less volatile than nominal bonds (Campbell, Shiller, & Viceira, 2009).

## 6.3 The Transformation in Corporate Debt Financing

Over the past few years, there has been massive growth in the issuance of corporate bonds in developing countries. This trend has been especially evident since the start of the global financial crisis, which has given many companies greater access to capital markets while exposing them to new financial risks. This pattern is particularly evident in conditions where laws are not firmly established. For example, the absence of clear rules can increase investor uncertainty, which is especially burdensome for companies.

Like other financial markets, the international corporate bond market has undergone significant changes in the last two decades. The average annual issuance (as a percentage of GDP) In the pre-crisis period, for all countries included in the sample, it was approximately 1.56% of GDP (2000–2007).

Despite the growing challenges, bonds have remained an important tool for raising money in many countries. This trend is linked to the economic boom prior to the GFC and can be considered a sustainable level of corporate borrowing under normal market conditions.

The corporate bond market was significantly affected by the GFC, resulting in a new phase of structure. Between 2008 and 2023, corporate bond issuance per annum grew by 0.85 percentage points relative to the pre-crisis years, reaching 2.41% of GDP. This move can be attributed to changes in the global financial system driven by low interest rates and quantitative easing implemented by leading central banks worldwide (Kashyap & Stein, 2023). In this industry, low-cost debt has become the rule of the day, and companies are using market debt to finance growth and refinance existing debt. The international issue is thus ever-growing.

As shown in Table 6.1, average global corporate bond issuance reached a pandemic-related peak of 2.97% of GDP across the sampled countries. This was a 0.56 percentage-point increase over 2019. That can be explained by the extreme liquidity crunch, during which corporations across the globe turned to bond markets to secure the funds they needed and stay afloat amid the global economic shutdown.

Corporate bond issuance, however, was short-lived. By 2023, the bond market had declined to approximately 2.50% of GDP.

This represents a 0.47-percentage-point decrease compared to the peak of the COVID-19 pandemic. This might be explained by central banks around the world raising interest rates to curb inflation, a major reason for

**Table 6.1** Analysis of global corporate bond trends across key periods

| *Period* | *Average Annual Issuance (as a Percentage of GDP)* | *Change vs. the Previous period* | *Some Key Markets Developments* |
|---|---|---|---|
| 2000–2007 | 1.56% | | Pre-crisis expansion |
| 2008–2023 | 2.41% | +0.85 ppt | Post-GFC/QE time |
| Pandemic Peak (2021) | 2.97% | +0.56 ppt (vs. 2019) | Emergency liquidity |
| 2023 | 2.48% | −0.47 ppt (vs. pandemic peak) | Rate hike cycle and normalization |

Notes: Americas: Argentina, Brazil, Canada, Chile, Costa Rica, Mexico, United States
Asia Pacific: Australia, China, Hong Kong, India, Japan, South Korea, New Zealand, Pakistan, Philippines
Europe: Austria, Belgium, Bulgaria, Croatia, Cyprus, Czech Republic, Denmark, Finland, France, Germany, Greece, Hungary, Ireland, Italy, Luxembourg, Malta, Netherlands, Poland, Portugal, Romania, Slovenia, Slovakia, Spain, United Kingdom.
Africa: South Africa, Nigeria, Egypt.
Source: Author's calculation and elaboration on the Global Financial Database

the decline. Subsequently, bond market activity has declined due to the shift toward more restrictive policies and the onset of a period of stabilization and standardization following the crisis.

Furthermore, comparative analysis of regional corporate bond issuance (as a percentage of GDP) is displayed in Table 6.2.

Table 6.2 shows significant heterogeneity in growth dynamics and crisis sensitivity of financial flows across the regions. Africa has experienced the highest growth rate over the last two decades, at 6.04% annually, but from a relatively low base. This data shows the region's dynamic capital market. The Americas are also experiencing consistent growth of 4.20%, with lower growth in the Asia Pacific at 3.09%. Europe registered only a slight annual growth rate of 1.38% because it has mature, developed financial markets. This not only indicates its maturity but also the traditional superiority of the banking sector over capital markets and corporate finance.

However, the medium-term indicators show different crisis effects across regions. For example, we found a negative effect of the GFC on the Americas and Africa and a positive effect on the Asia Pacific and Europe. The picture splits when viewed over ten years. To illustrate, Europe (+ 2.77%) and Asia Pacific (+1.36%) recorded moderate growth, whereas the Americas (-2.45%) and Africa (-3.01%) showed declines (Table 6.2). This shows a sharp decline compared with past decades. As a result of the

**Table 6.2** The impact of the crisis on corporate bond market development

| | *Annualized Growth (%)* | *Peak Value/Country* | *5Y CAGR (%) (2017–2022)* | *10Y CAGR (%) (2012–2022)* | *GFC impact (2008–09 vs. 2006–07)* | *COVID-19 Impact (2020 vs. 2019)* |
|---|---|---|---|---|---|---|
| America | 4.2% | U.S, 7.28% (2020), Canada 4.97% (2017) | −0.37 | −2.45 | −0.61 ppt | +0.74 ppt |
| Europe | 1.38% | Belgium, 13.57% (2016), Netherland 5.41% (2020); Croatia, 5.29% (2013); the U.K., 5.04% (2020) | −2.34 | 2.77 | +0.29 ppt | +0.40 ppt |
| Asia Pacific | 3.09% | Hong Kong, 7.57% (2012); China, 6.39% (2016); New Zealand, 4.5 % | −2.99 | 1.36 | +0.81 ppt | +0.43 ppt |
| Africa | 6.04% | South Africa 2.17% (2022) | −2.94 | −3.01 | −0.32 ppt | +0.86 ppt |

Notes: Americas: Argentina, Brazil, Canada, Chile, Costa Rica, Mexico, and the United States
Asia Pacific: Australia, China, Hong Kong, India, Japan, South Korea, New Zealand, Pakistan, and the Philippines
Europe: Austria, Belgium, Bulgaria, Croatia, Cyprus, Czech Republic, Denmark, Finland, France, Germany, Greece, Hungary, Ireland, Italy, Luxembourg, Malta, Netherlands, Poland, Portugal, Romania, Slovenia, Slovakia, Spain, and the United Kingdom.
Africa: South Africa, Nigeria, and Egypt.
Source: Author's calculation and elaboration on the Global Financial Database

COVID-19 pandemic, some regions experienced an unexpected increase in bond issuance. Africa experienced the largest effect, recording an increase of +0.86 percent. Increased financing needs and changed liquidity requirements clearly support this surge.

The comparison with key years and the values of the largest outstanding bond issues presents specifics of the financial markets in the regions. The European region is characterized by a high degree of heterogeneity, with a few idiosyncratic peaks, including Belgium (13.57% in 2016) and Croatia (5.29% in 2013), reflecting the unequal integration of regional capital markets.

The Americas and Asia-Pacific markets have higher concentration and relative stability. Major economic centers such as the United States, Canada, China, and Hong Kong are associated with the largest outstanding amount of bond issues. This implies the existence of more liquid and developed capital markets in these countries. By comparison, Africa remains in the early stages of corporate bond market development, with a relatively low level of 2.17% (South Africa, 2022) (Table 6.2).

Based on the above, it may be concluded that the European market is more fragmented and volatile than those of America and Asia, indicating the complexity and unevenness of its internal structure. The response to the crisis has been mixed across world regions. Asia and the Pacific have been the most vulnerable to the GFC. The COVID-19 pandemic has led to a global increase in the outstanding amount of bond issues. The largest increases in the outstanding amount of bond issues were in Africa (+ 0.86 p.p.) and the Americas (+0.74 p.p.), indicating that firms worldwide resorted to bond markets as an important source of liquidity during large, sudden shocks. Global corporate bond markets exhibit significant regional differences in risks and opportunities. While resilient and having successfully coped with COVID-19, Africa remains the most vulnerable market due to weak bond performances and low market depth. As Europe has been heterogeneous, the Asia-Pacific region has grown over the past decade with increasing market depth. The Americas region has seen cyclical market oscillations, periods of strong growth, and several market contractions. Overall, recent developments indicate a global slowdown in growth dynamics fueled by rising interest rates, posing new challenges for corporate financing worldwide.

## 6.4 The New Geography and Dynamics of Corporate Finance

The analysis of long-term concentration in the corporate bond market reveals significant structural changes in the international financial market. Between 2000 and 2007, the U.S. market accounted for 49.9% of the total market share in the Americas. This indicates a high level of regional concentration. At the same time, China held a modest 9.6% in the Asia-Pacific region, while Germany, in a highly fragmented Europe, accounted for 15.8% of the market share (Table 6.3).

**Table 6.3** Regional analysis of corporate bond issuance concentration

| *Region* | *Key Country* | *Period of 2000–07* | *Period of 2008–23* | *Pandemic Peak* |
|---|---|---|---|---|
| Americas | U.S. | 49.90% | 39.20% | 43.10% |
| Asia Pacific | China | 9.60% | 35.80% | 29.60% |
| Europa | Germany | 15.8% | 13.50% | 15.30% |

Note: Americas: Argentina, Brazil, Canada, Chile, Costa Rica, Mexico, and the United States
Asia Pacific: Australia, China, Hong Kong, India, Japan, South Korea, New Zealand, Pakistan, and the Philippines.
Europe: Austria, Belgium, Bulgaria, Croatia, Cyprus, Czech Republic, Denmark, Finland, France, Germany, Greece, Hungary, Ireland, Italy, Luxembourg, Malta, Netherlands, Poland, Portugal, Romania, Slovenia, Slovakia, Spain, and the United Kingdom.
Source: Author's calculation and elaboration on the Global Financial Development Database

After the GFC, concentration patterns have changed and evolved. Namely, due to diversification and growth in the corporate bond market, the US share in its region decreased to 39.2% between 2008 and 2023, as markets in other countries in the Americas, especially Brazil and Canada, grew. With a 35.8% share of the outstanding volume of its corporate bond issuance between 2008 and 2023, Asia has emerged as a new center of financial power and an important learner on the global stage. Nevertheless, Germany holds a stable 13.5% share of the European market, indicating that the European capital market remains heterogeneous. The COVID-19 pandemic is the main reason for the continuous decline in the capital market. The current capital market downturns are largely due to the COVID-19 pandemic. For example, the share of the outstanding volume of corporate bond issuance in the United States fell to 43.1% during COVID-19, while China's share in Asia remained stable around 29.6% (see Table 6.3). However, Germany has maintained its position, with a modest increase to 15.3%. These results clearly indicate a shift in the world's epicenters of the corporate bond market, as China becomes more important in Asia. For example, China's bond market is the second largest worldwide, with a total of $24.6 trillion in 2024 (U.S. Department of State, 2025). At the same time, the United States remains a reliable haven throughout the crisis.

Further, a decoupling analysis was conducted to explore whether individual national bond markets have begun to act more independently of the United States (Table 6.4). To this end, we shall determine the beta

**Table 6.4** Analysis of the decoupling process in the corporate bond market

| *Region* | *2001–2008* | *2011–2022* | *Change* | *Explanation* |
|---|---|---|---|---|
| Americas | 0.85 | 0.92 | +0.07 | Less decoupling |
| Europa | 0.62 | 0.45 | −0.17 | Decoupling |
| Asia Pacific | 0.78 | 0.41 | −0.37 | Strong decoupling |
| China | 0.71 | 0.28 | −0.43 | Strongest decoupling |

Note: Americas: Argentina, Brazil, Canada, Chile, Costa Rica, and Mexico (excluding the United States) Asia Pacific: Australia, China, Hong Kong, India, Japan, South Korea, New Zealand, Pakistan, and the Philippines.

Europe: Austria, Belgium, Bulgaria, Croatia, Cyprus, Czech Republic, Denmark, Finland, France, Germany, Greece, Hungary, Ireland, Italy, Luxembourg, Malta, Netherlands, Poland, Portugal, Romania, Slovenia, Slovakia, Spain, and the United Kingdom.

Africa: South Africa, Nigeria, and Egypt.

Source: Author's calculation and elaboration on the Global Financial Development Database

coefficient for the periods prior to the GFC (2001–2008) and after the GFC (2011–2022).

In this context, the beta coefficient measures how the regional bond market reacts to changes in the US market. Lower beta values suggest that bonds move less in sync with the U.S. market, indicating greater decoupling.

In the last 20 years, the process of decoupling or the separation of market movements has been observed. More specifically, the global dynamics of corporate bonds have undergone a fundamental structural change. The statistics clearly indicate that other national financial markets have gradually been acting more independently of the U.S. market. China is the most striking example of such change. Although the Chinese market exhibited a strong relationship in the pre-GFC crisis period ($\beta = 0.71$), in the post-GFC crisis period, the relationship was much weaker ($\beta = 0.28$; Table 6.4).

China is not the only nation to follow this trend. Other countries in the Asia-Pacific region have followed a similar trend. For example, these countries have seen dependence drop from 0.71 to 0.41, a decline of about 42%, while European countries have seen it drop from 0.62 to 0.45, a decline of about 27%. This suggests that regional capital markets are becoming increasingly autonomous and developing their own dynamics, influencing the global reorganization of financial ties.

However, this phenomenon of decoupling does not apply equally to all countries. The rest of the US remains firmly tied to the American market,

**Table 6.5** Analysis of corporate bond market volatility

| *Region* | *Average (% GDP)* | *St. Deviation* | *Coefficient of Variation (CV)* |
|---|---|---|---|
| Europe | 1.9% | 0.58% | 31.6% |
| Africa | 0.6% | 0.34% | 58% |
| Americas | 2.13% | 0.65% | 30.4% |
| Asia Pacific | 1.94% | 0.62% | 31.6% |

Note: Americas: Argentina, Brazil, Canada, Chile, Costa Rica, Mexico, and the United States
Asia Pacific: Australia, China, Hong Kong, India, Japan, South Korea, New Zealand, Pakistan, and the Philippines.
Europe: Austria, Belgium, Bulgaria, Croatia, Cyprus, Czech Republic, Denmark, Finland, France, Germany, Greece, Hungary, Ireland, Italy, Luxembourg, Malta, Netherlands, Poland, Portugal, Romania, Slovenia, Slovakia, Spain, and the United Kingdom.
Africa: South Africa, Nigeria, and Egypt.
Source: Author's calculation and elaboration on the Global Financial Development Database

and that connection has grown even stronger. This highlights how important geographical proximity and strong economic ties are to maintaining regional integration. As a result, the global corporate bond market is undergoing a significant change. The American financial market, which for decades was at the center of global finance, is now seeing the rise of independent regional powers. The decoupling is most noticeable in Asia, where China is emerging as an important player in the global financial system. The implications of this change for future capital flows, risk management, and the development of global economic centers are significant (Witt et al., 2023).

We also conducted an analysis to determine which corporate bond market was the most volatile. To do this, we calculated the standard deviation values for each region over the entire analysis period (Table 6.5).

Corporate bond market volatility analysis shows a major disparity in stability across regions over the last 20 years. Given the varying initial levels of capital market development across the globe, we used the coefficient of variation (CV) to obtain a comparable estimate of financial market volatility.

The African market showed the highest relative volatility with a coefficient of variation of 58%. Although the average bond issuance is low (0.6% of GDP), the combination of a small base and sudden jumps in issuance in individual countries led to a pronounced volatility, typical of markets in the early stages of development. Europe showed somewhat lower, but still high volatility (CV = 31.6%).

In Europe, the corporate bond market is fragmented, where extreme events in individual countries, such as the recapitalization of Belgian banks, significantly affect regional averages (CV=31%). Also, the U.S. corporate bond market, with an average issuance-to-GDP ratio of 2.13% and a coefficient of variation of 30.4%, exhibits a similar level of stability (Table 6.5). Similarly, Asia Pacific (CV = 31.6%) and Europe (CV = 31%) show comparable stability. These findings highlight that, despite different market structures—fragmented Europe versus China-led Asia—both regions offer similar predictability to investors. This result points to a gradual, disciplined expansion and deepening integration of regional capital markets. Overall, the findings clearly confirm that the degree of market development and financial integration is directly reflected in its stability.

## 6.5 Conclusion

The global corporate bond market has undergone a profound transformation since the GFC. This change is evident in a consistent rise in bond issuance and a shift in financial influence. In pre-GFC crises, there was a steady trend toward sustainable borrowing worldwide, but the post-crisis era of low interest rates and quantitative easing has established a new normal. Corporate bond issuance plays a key role in corporate financing, with issuance levels steadily increasing. The distribution of corporate debt varies by region, with the United States being the largest debt issuer, and Africa remains a peripheral market.

Similarly, the Asia-Pacific region, led by China, is emerging as a new financial hub with strong growth and increasing financial independence from the US. Meanwhile, Europe has proven to be a mature yet fragmented market, with its stability undermined by uneven integration. Finally, Africa, despite being the fastest-growing market due to its small initial base, shows the greatest volatility and remains in the early stages of development.

Certain developments in financial markets suggest that regional markets are becoming less reliant on the US financial cycle. For example, China is building its own financial system. As a result, the corporate bond market is shifting from a solely American model to a more multipolar structure, providing companies easier access to global capital. However, this transition also introduces increased instability, regional division, and heightened vulnerability to monetary policies and global crises.

The notable decline in China's beta (from 0.71 to 0.28) within the US corporate cycle challenges the notion that the US and China are not competitors (Winecoff, 2020; Starrs, 2019).

Our assessment indicates that the new duopoly, which controls 55.6% of global financial assets, is characterized by a shift in financial influence away from traditional Western centers towards a balanced US-China dynamic. This differs from the debate about whether China is trying to moderate or reduce U.S. expansion. Financial centers adapt to current market conditions through diversification, while IFCs maintain their structural role. Ultimately, this is a realm where tension or instability is not tied to stocks; instead, the focus is on dominance and capital allocation strategies.

## References


–Campbell, J.Y., Shiller, R.J., & Viceira, L.M. (2009). Understanding inflation-indexed bond markets. Brookings Papers on Economic Activity, Spring 2009. Harvard University, National Bureau of Economic Research.

–Chen, Z., Mao, C.X., & Wang, Y. (2010). Why firms issue callable bonds: Hedging investment uncertainty. Journal of Corporate Finance, 16(4), 588–607. https://doi.org/10.1016/j.jcorpfin.2010.06.003

–Chen, F., Huang, J.-Z., Sun, Z., & Yu, T. (2020). Why do firms issue guaranteed bonds? Journal of Banking & Finance, 119, 105396. https://doi.org/10.1016/j.jbankfin.2018.08.002

–Choudhry, M. (2006). An Introduction to Bond Markets, Third Edition, John Wiley & Sons Ltd.

–Connolly, K. (1998). Pricing Convertible Bonds. John Wiley & Sons, Chichester, UK.

–Fabozzi, F. (ed.) (2002). The Handbook of Fixed Income Securities (6th edn). McGraw-Hill, Princeton, NJ.

–Kashyap, A.K., & Stein, J.C. (2023). Monetary policy is when the central bank shapes financial-market sentiment. Journal of Economic Perspectives, 37(1), 53–76.

–Levinson, M. (2010). Guide to Financial Markets: Why they exist and how they work, Fifth edition, The Economist Newspaper Ltd.

–Litzenberger, R. H., Beaglehole, D. R., and Reynolds, C. E. (1996). Assessing Catastrophe-Reinsurance-Linked Securities as a New Asset Class. The Journal of Portfolio Management, (76–86). DOI: https://doi.org/10.3905/jpm.1996.076

–McConnel, J. J. and E. S. Schwartz, 1986, "LYONS Taming", Journal of Finance, vol. 41, no. 3, pp. 561–576.

–Neftci, S. N., & Santos, A. O. (2003). Puttable and extendible bonds: Developing interest rate derivatives for emerging markets (IMF Working Paper No. 2003/201, p. 30). International Monetary Fund. https://doi.org/10.5089/9781451874372.001

–Pilbeam, K. (2010), Finance and Financial Markets, Third issue, Palgrave.

–Starrs, S. K. (2018). Can China unmake the American making of global capitalism? *Socialist Register*, *55*, 173–200. https://socialistregister.com/index.php/srv/article/view/30942/23349

–Stowell, D. P. (2018). Sundaresan, S. (2009). Fixed Income Markets and Their Derivatives, Third Edition, Elsevier Inc.

–Stuart, M., and Kari, K. (2002). Innovative Financial Instruments for Natural Disaster Risk Management. Sustainable Development Department Technical Papers Series. Retrieved from https://www.researchgate.net/publication/254421641_Innovative_Financial_Instruments_for_Natural_Disaster_Risk_Management

–U.S. Department of State. (2025). 2025 Investment Climate Statements: China, U.S. Department of State, https://www.state.gov/reports/2025-investment-climate-statements/china

–US SEC (2014), Securities and Exchange Commission, Investor Bulletin, http://www.sec.gov/investor/alerts/municipalbondsbulletin.pdf Accessed on 28 May 2014.

–Winecoff, W. K. (2020). The persistent myth of lost hegemony, revisited: Structural power as a complex network phenomenon. *European Journal of International Relations*, *26*(1), 209–252. https://doi.org/10.1177/1354066120952876

–Witt, M. A., Lewin, A. Y., Li, P. P., & Gaur, A. (2023). Decoupling in international business: Evidence, drivers, impact, and implications for IB research. Journal of World Business, 58(1), 101399.

CHAPTER 7

# The Great Rebalancing: A Comparative Study of Global Capital Market Structures

**Abstract** This chapter provides a quantitative analysis of global capital markets for 2000-2023, based on three interconnected dimensions that enable a comprehensive examination of the structural development and dynamics of modern financial systems. This chapter explores the structure and health of capital markets under four pillars, such as depth, efficiency, breadth, and volatility, with differences between the dynamic Asia Pacific and the developed markets of Europe, the Americas, and Africa. It then compares the processes of raising capital: equity issuance is highly sensitive to the cycle, whereas debt is relatively insensitive and more deterministic (SIFMA, Refinitiv LSEG, Dealogic). Finally, the global fixed-income market is assessed (BIS, IMF), and the US-China duopoly is seen as emerging at the expense of the US-EU-Japan triumvirate.

**Keywords** Equity markets • Derivative markets • Fixed-income markets • Crisis impact (GFC/COVID-19) • Regional analysis



M. Ganić, *Structural Change and Competitive Dynamics in Global Financial Markets*,
https://doi.org/10.1007/978-3-032-28906-3_7

## 7.1 Introduction

Financial markets have changed radically since the beginning of the century. The GFC crisis highlighted that financial globalization is accelerating and spreading contagion evenly across economies (Beck et al., 2009). The COVID-19 pandemic has unsettled investors (Li et al., 2022), with many fearing that their previously stable investment portfolios may change. This would have a major impact not only on individual investors' portfolios but also on the overall structure of institutional investors' portfolios (Atri et al., 2021). It has had far-reaching implications and struck a hard blow to the global economy and its stock markets, as has been the case in past crises, which react first. This fall has reminded us of the magnitude of the GFC (Hassan & Riveros Gavilanes, 2021). The COVID-19 pandemic has made financial markets much more interconnected than in other crises (So et al., 2021). Both the first and second waves of the COVID-19 pandemic led to spillover volatility and contagion between the Chinese and US stock markets. However, in the US, there is a persistent relationship among yield movements, uncertainty, and the course of the pandemic (Yousfi et al., 2021).

Ali et al.'s (2020) study showed that almost all financial instruments, except US government bonds, experienced increased volatility and negative returns. This suggests that investors used risk-free instruments to reduce their risk appetite during the COVID-19 pandemic. The latest wave of the global financial crisis was also triggered by the pandemic, leading to significant capital flows and declines in real estate prices across most global markets (Adekoya & Oliyide, 2021). As Zhao et al. (2023) have shown, developed countries have a greater impact on financial markets due to reduced supply and demand and more stable economies.

The methodology involves a quantitative analysis of global financial market trends from 2000 to 2022, with a focus on equity and derivative markets from 2009 to 2023. Financial depth, efficiency, breadth, and volatility are the four key components of financial market development that this study focuses on. A CAGR and comparative comparisons of four world regions (the Americas, Europe, Asia Pacific, and Africa) are used to measure dynamics and long-term trends in the financial market. Special focus is given to the impact of two crisis periods, the GFC crisis and the COVID-19 pandemic, in the period before and after these crises. To assess the market's ability to allocate capital and transfer risk, the method involves analyzing capital issuance activity (equity and debt) and derivative markets, using factors such as issuance value, number of transactions, and regional concentration.

## 7.2 Regional Implications of the Financial Market's Development: Depth and Volatility

This part uses a quantitative approach to examine four major dimensions of the capital market, including depth, efficiency, breadth, and volatility, in four different regions around the world during the years 2000 through 2022. A CAGR can be calculated using data from the World Bank's Global Financial Development Database. These calculations aim to analyze long-term trends, including regional differences and year-to-year fluctuations, and to predict how these figures might behave during a crisis. Market liquidity and depth depend on the total stock market trading volume and GDP. The market's relative activity determines the liquidity and depth of a financial market. The study of this indicator across 31 countries from 2000 to 2022 shows diverse paths of financial market development and, at the same time, conflicting responses to the global financial crisis (Table 7.1).

The Asia-Pacific region has become an independent driver of global liquidity growth. The region's deepening capital markets, as in Hong Kong and China, resulted in growth, with trading volume sufficient to

**Table 7.1** Regional depth analysis of the stock market

| *Region* | *Latest Y/Y △ (2021–22)* | *5Y CAGR* | *10Y CAGR* | *Annualized Growth (2000–2022)* | *Average (2000–2022)* | *GFC Impact (2008–09 vs. 2006–2007)* | *COVID-19 Impact (2020 vs. 2019)* |
|---|---|---|---|---|---|---|---|
| America | −0.1 p.p. | 6.42% | 4.12% | 2.38% | 54.20% | +11.2 p.p. | +16.4 p.p. |
| Europe | −3.6 p.p. | 2.91% | 2.45% | −0.02% | 93.80% | −2.8 p.p. | +5.3 p.p. |
| Asia Pacific | −10.0 p.p. | 4.72% | 4.68% | 5.21% | 158.30% | −10.5 p.p. | +27.3 p.p. |
| Africa | +1.2 p.p. | 7.28% | 6.82% | 4.51% | 23.50% | −4.2 p.p. | +5.2 p.p. |

Note: The sample includes the following countries: America (Argentina, Brazil, Canada, Chile, Costa Rica, Mexico, and the United States); Europe (Austria, Belgium, Denmark, Finland, France, Germany, Greece, Ireland, Italy, the Netherlands, Portugal, Spain, Sweden, and the United Kingdom); Asia Pacific (Australia, China, Hong Kong, India, Japan, South Korea, New Zealand, Pakistan, and the Philippines); Africa (South Africa)

Source: Author's calculation based on The World Bank's Global Financial Development Database account for 158.3% of regional GDP and an annual growth rate of 5.21% over 2000–2021. This contrasts with the long-term decline in liquidity in Europe. In contrast to the Asia-Pacific region, Europe has experienced a long-term decline in capital market liquidity, with an average decrease of -0.22% since the dot-com era.

The GFC affected the Americas the most, with an 11.2-percentage-point reduction in liquidity. In the meantime, the Asia-Pacific region recorded a 10.5-percentage-point decline during the same period. Liquidity in Europe decreased to 0.7 from 2.8, while liquidity in Africa decreased slightly.

The COVID-19 pandemic reversed these trends, increasing liquidity across all regions. The Asia-Pacific region recorded the largest increase, growing by an impressive 27.3 percentage points, followed by the United States (16.4 percentage points), Europe (5.3 percentage points), and Africa (5.2 percentage points). Africa showed a current annual growth rate of 7.28% from 2017 to 2022, significantly exceeding growth in the Americas (6.42%), Asia (4.72%), and Europe (2.91%). Africa maintains the lead with a CAGR of 6.82% over the tenth period (2012–2022), while the Americas, Asia Pacific, and Europe are at 4.12%, 4.68%, and 2.45%, respectively (see Table 7.1).

The United Kingdom has, however, experienced a consistent and high degree of market depth—above 95% of GDP on average over the years 2016–2022—and has exhibited a swift and robust recovery following the global financial crisis, with the most dependable outcomes in Europe by 2022 (underlying data from the World Bank's Global Financial Development Database). Overall, Europe has moved from being one of the world's most liquid capital markets in 2000 to a mature yet weak market that has not yet recovered to the heights of the dot-com days. This experience shows the European market's sensitivity to financial shocks and its slower recovery compared with more agile competitors in Asia and the Americas.

The Americas' capital market can be viewed through the lens of two dominant players. First, the United States remains a reliable anchor in the region, with the largest and most liquid market, and has demonstrated great strength in the face of the GFC. The trend, however, over the long run, indicates a minor decrease in relative liquidity compared to the economy's size. Secondly, the key growth engine is Brazil; the value of trade has grown from 14.35% of GDP in 2000 to 94.82% in 2022 (data from the World Bank's Global Financial Development Database), demonstrating the rapid increase in the country's integration into global financial flows. Canada has a mature, stable level of market depth and tends to rank only second to the US. On the other hand, Mexico and Argentina have experienced a long-term liquidity squeeze, which is also pushing them out of regional leadership and global competitiveness.

There have been sharp contrasts between regional responses to the two major crises of this century. America was the worst hit by the GFC, with liquidity decreasing by over 11.2 percentage points, while Asia Pacific recorded a decline of 10.5 percentage points during the same period. Europe experienced a modest 2.8-percentage-point decline, and Africa saw a 4.2-percentage-point decline. During COVID-19, the highest growth in liquidity was 27.3 percentage points in the Asia Pacific. America was followed by 16.4 percentage points, Europe by 5.3 percentage points, and Africa by 5.2 percentage points.

Additionally, stock market efficiency, as measured by the turnover ratio, has been analyzed as a proxy for volatility. The Asia-Pacific region leads globally, with the highest average turnover of 117.6% between 2000 and 2022, rising to 148.3% since 2015. Trading in China has been a major driver of this performance, with South Korea and India the other most efficient markets. Very high trading volumes in China drive this performance,

**Table 7.2** Analysis of stock market efficiency (turnover ratio) by region

| *Region* | *Average Turnover (All Years)* | *Average Turnover (Post-2015)* | *Efficiency Year Peak* | *Peak Efficiency Value* | *2022 value* | *COVID-19 Impact (2020 vs. 2019)* |
|---|---|---|---|---|---|---|
| America | 51.06 | 45.22 | 2008 | 207.6 (U.S) | 54.4 | +14 p.p. |
| Europe | 95.82 | 63.1 | 2007 | 163.2 (U.K.) | 64.1 | +2.9 p.p. |
| Asia Pacific | 117.62 | 148.3 | 2015 | 300 (China) | 160.4 | +24.9 p.p. |
| Africa | 33.55 | 30.78 | 2008 | 42 (South Africa) | 32.8 | +3 p.p. |

Note: The sample includes the following countries: America (Argentina, Brazil, Canada, Chile, Costa Rica, Mexico, and the United States); Europe (Austria, Belgium, Denmark, France, Germany, Greece, Ireland, Italy, the Netherlands, Portugal, Sweden, and the United Kingdom); Asia Pacific (Australia, China, Hong Kong, India, Japan, South Korea, New Zealand, Pakistan, and the Philippines); Africa (South Africa)

Finland and Spain are excluded as outliers.

Source: Author's calculation based on The World Bank's Global Financial Development Database while South Korea and India are also among the most efficient markets. Despite the downturn from the record peak of 300% in 2015 (China), the 103.4% figure in 2022 still shows that the number of stocks in the area is being turned over annually, indicating a significant culture of active trading. The region experienced the greatest impact of COVID-19, with turnover increasing by 24.9 percentage points in 2020. (Table 7.2).

The US capital market is highly efficient but still highly volatile. The long-term turnover of 51.1% is substantial, and the US and Canada represent the most liquid and most important markets, but Brazil is gaining momentum. Crisis responses have been intense: during the GFC, the U.S. turnover peaked at 207.6%, and the COVID-19 pandemic caused a 14.0-percentage-point increase — the second-largest globally after Asia Pacific. These movements demonstrate that investors will quickly enter new speculative positions in a panic. The fall to 54.4% in 2022 indicates a cooling market following the real rush seen in 2020–2021 (Table 7.2).

There is a mix of structural weakness and stability in the European capital market. The turnover rate since 2015 (63.1%) is significantly lower than the pre-crisis level (163.2% in 2007), suggesting a shift toward high-frequency trading rather than long-term buy-and-hold investing.

Africa, represented by South Africa, has relatively low liquidity in its financial markets. The average turnover ratio is 33.6% over the long term and 30.8% since 2015. Such developments indicate a more stable and less volatile market but also reflect lower trading intensity and limited market activity. The turnover ratio for 2022 was 32.8%, which is roughly in line with the long-term average for Africa (Table 7.2).

Market volatility, as measured by the turnover ratio, varies significantly across regions and crises. This shows that greater market efficiency (higher turnover) or a higher number of transactions usually leads to greater market volatility, especially in more developed and liquid financial markets. Conversely, markets that are more stable and less liquid experience fewer fluctuations.

Next, to measure equity market breadth and accessibility for a population, we use the indicator "Number of listed companies per 1,000,000 people" (from the World Bank's Global Financial Development Database). The number of listed companies per capita shows a global imbalance: the Americas, Europe, and Africa have been in steady decline since 2000, with annualized growth rates of -2.37%, -4.17%, and -2.15%, respectively, whereas Asia recorded a growth of 3.43% annually over the same period

**Table 7.3** Regional analysis of equity market breadth

| *Region* | *Annualized Growth (2000–2022)* | *Peak year* | *Peak value in $B* | *5Y CAGR* | *10Y CAGR* | *GFC impact (2008–09 vs. 2006–2007)* | *COVID-19 impact (2020 vs. 2019)* |
|---|---|---|---|---|---|---|---|
| Americas | −2.37% | 2000 | 14.6 | −2.17% | −2.43% | −0.55 | −0.2 |
| Europe | −4.17% | 2000 | 27.6 | −3.93% | −4.65% | −1.7 | −0.4 |
| Asia Pacific | 3.43% | 2022 | 74.7 | 4.27% | 3.97% | 2.8 | 2.8 |
| Africa | −2.15% | 2000 | 13.43 | −2.15% | −2.12% | −0.48 | −0.19 |

Source: Author's calculation based on World Bank (2023): The World Bank's Global Financial Development Database

(Table 7.3). The GFC worldwide exacerbated the shrinkage, especially in Europe (-1.7 percentage points), whereas COVID-19 has had little effect, which supports the view that this is a long-term trend rather than a shock. This process reflects industry concentration, where major players become more dominant, along with a shift towards market privatization and regulatory barriers that hinder new listings.

The Americas have experienced a steady decline in the breadth of capital markets, with an average annual decline of 2.37% since their high in 2000. The 5-year CAGR of the region was -2.17 from 2017 to 2022 and -2.43 from 2012 to 2022 (Table 7.3). Although developed economies such as the US and Canada have high absolute numbers, in others, the number of listed companies has dropped by half (from 24.5 to 12.6 per million people in the US). Latin America also scores low relative to the regional average, with ratios consistently below it and declining. This indicates the influence of structural forces, including market consolidation, the shift towards private equity, and regulatory barriers to new listings.

Capital market contraction has been most pronounced in Europe, where the average annual decline has been -4.17% since 2000, with 5-year and 10-year CAGR declines of -3.93% and -4.65%, respectively (Table 7.3). Nearly all the largest economies, such as Germany, France, and the United Kingdom, showed long-term declines, with Spain particularly notable for its steep decline from extremely high initial levels (underlying data from the World Bank's Global Financial Development Database). The GFC continued this trend, narrowing the market range by 1.7 percentage points, and COVID-19 caused a slight decrease to -0.4 percent. These indicators show how structural forces, including industrial concentration, corporate privatization, and the regulatory environment, are driving large incumbent players and new entrants into the market.

The Asia-Pacific region is the exact opposite of global market consolidation, with stable growth of +3.43% per year since 2000 and a fast-growing public capital market. In 2022, there were 74.7 companies per million people in the region. Over the past five years, growth has been at a 5-year CAGR of 4.27%, and over the past ten years, at a 10-year CAGR of 3.97%. For example, Australia has a stable base, and China—the most dynamic—has been growing exponentially from a low starting point. These tendencies are associated with robust economic growth, favorable policies, the growing role of public capital markets as a growth engine, and greater reputation and openness to investment by the general populace.

The market efficiency analysis using the turnover ratio reveals a regional difference. However, it is also necessary to consider the performance of the leading indices. Table 7.4 illustrates the trend of key global indices, which validates the technological superiority of the USA (S&P 500 10-year CAGR: 9.9%) and the fragility of European markets outside Germany and France.

With a 10-year CAGR of -3.1%, Hong Kong's Hang Seng Index has declined significantly, with a total loss of 40% from 2021 to 2023. Although general data on the regional market do not indicate obvious geopolitical risks or a decline in the Chinese economy, this still suggests otherwise. In contrast, Japan's Nikkei 225 achieved an impressive 5-year CAGR of 10.8%, making it the leader in the Asian market, driven by successful

**Table 7.4** Major stock market indices of the major global stock markets

| *Index* | *2023 level* | *10Y CAGR* | *5Y CAGR* | *2023 YoY* | *Peak level (Year)* | *Crisis impact* |
|---|---|---|---|---|---|---|
| S&P 500 | 4,769.83 | 9.90% | 13.70% | 24.20% | 4,766.18 (2021) | –19% (2022) |
| S&P/TSX | 20,958.44 | 4.40% | 7.90% | 8.10% | 21,222.84 (2021) | -9% (2022) |
| CAC40 | 7,543.18 | 5.80% | 9.80% | 16.50% | 7,153.03 (2021) | –10% (2022) |
| DAX | 16,751.64 | 5.80% | 9.70% | 20.30% | 15,884.86 (2021) | –12% (2022) |
| Hang Seng | 17,047.39 | –3.10% | -8.00% | –13.80% | 33,154.12 (2018) | –40% (2021–2023) |
| Nikkei 225 | 33,464.17 | 7.50% | 10.80% | 28.20% | 33,464.17 (2023) | -9% (2022) |
| FTSE 100 | 7,733.24 | 1.40% | 2.80% | 3.80% | 7,903.50 (2023) | –11% (2022) |

Source: Author's elaboration on SIFMA Capital Markets Fact Book (2024), based on data from Refinitiv LSEG Data & Analytics, Dealogic, Bloomberg, S&P Global, national stock exchanges, and World Bank corporate reforms. The indicators in Table 7.4 show that the Asia-Pacific region had the best market efficiency (166.8% compared to 2015).

Also, global capital markets have experienced strong long-term growth despite cyclical fluctuations. The US S&P 500 was up front, with an impressive 10-year CAGR of 9.9%, nearly twice that of the top European indices, DAX (Germany) and CAC 40 (France; 5.8%), and by far exceeding the FTSE 100 (U.K.) which remained stagnant at 1.4%. Corporate reforms saw the Nikkei 225 in Japan perform the best in decades in the Asian market, with a 5-year CAGR of 7.5%.

In comparison, the Hang Seng Index of Hong Kong fell 3.1% over the 5 years (CAGR), with a 13.8% decline in 2023 alone, indicating a deceleration in the Chinese economy and geopolitical uncertainty. The US is leading because of the development of the technology industry, which reached its highest level in S&P 500 history, at 4,769.83 points in 2023 (+24.2% compared to the previous year).

The European DAX (Germany) and CAC 40 (France) indices recorded high returns in 2023 (+20.3% and +16.5%) in contrast to the humbler growth of the commodity markets, including the TSX in Canada (10Y CAGR of 4.4%) and the FTSE 100 in the U.K. (CAGR of 2.8%), despite the crisis environment (Table 7.4).

## 7.3 Capital Markets and Derivatives: Issuance Activity and Risk Transfer

This section relies on the quantitative analysis of international equity and debt issuance activity in 2009–2023 as the methodology. The primary indicators are the value of issuances per year, the number of issues, the CAGR over five and ten years, and the year-over-year changes, all calculated from raw data in the SIFMA Capital Markets Fact Book, which draws on Refinitiv LSEG Data and Analytics and Dealogic.

The statistics in Table 7.5 demonstrate the dynamic transformation of world capital markets over the last decade. Capital raising is primarily through debt issuance, averaging 5,300 issues annually, compared with 2,059 equity issues annually. Direct debt accounts for 95% of total debt, with an average of 5,048 issues annually. Although convertibles have a low market share, they are very volatile, falling in 2023 by 69.8% following a post-COVID-19 slump but gaining over 5 and 10 years with high CAGRs of 7.68% and 8.43%, respectively.

**Table 7.5** Global issuance activity (2009–2023)

| *($ Billions)* | *Avg Annual (2009–2023) in $B* | *Peak Year (Value) in $B* | *2023 YoY* | *5Y CAGR* | *10Y CAGR* | *Crisis Impact (2022)* |
|---|---|---|---|---|---|---|
| **By Region** | | | | | | |
| United States | $215.7 | 2021 ($376.4) | 46.20% | 8.48% | 5.99% | –77% |
| China | $101.1 | 2021 ($172.2) | –29.60% | 8.45% | –4.28% | –46% |
| EU | $95.9 | 2015 ($122.2) | 32.70% | 1.60% | 2.17% | –50% |
| Japan | $16.4 | 2023 ($34.0) | 324% | 11.54% | 0.13% | –74% |
| Emerging Markets | $118.1 | 2021 ($131.1) | –18.80% | 11.03% | 3.52% | –36% |
| Developed Markets | $13.9 | 2021 ($20.1) | –7.80% | 6.10% | 5.79% | –51% |
| Global Total | $529.0 | 2021 ($1,051) | 3.30% | 2.09% | 0.05% | –61% |
| **By Instrument Type** | | | | | | |
| Straight Debt | $5,048 | 2021 ($6,100) | 6.30% | 2.72% | 0.27% | –27% |
| Convertible Debt | $252 | 2021 ($444) | –69.8% | 7.68% | 8.43% | –58% |
| Total Debt | $5,300 | 2021 ($6,412) | 7.90% | 2.87% | 0.59% | –29% |
| Common Stock | $2,005 | 2021 ($3,703) | 6.20% | –5.21% | –4.40% | –39% |
| Preferred Stock | $54 | 2017 ($99) | –47.80% | 29.08% | 21.91% | –10% |
| Total Equity | $2,059 | 2021 ($3,740) | 5.60% | –4.86% | –3.91% | –39% |
| Total Issuance | $7,358 | 2021 ($10,152) | 7.10% | 0.58% | –0.69% | –33% |

Note: China: mainland only
Source: Author's elaboration on SIFMA Capital Markets Fact Book (2024), based on data from Refinitiv LSEG Data & Analytics, Dealogic, Bloomberg, S&P Global, national stock exchanges, and World Bank

Regional trends vary significantly. For example, the US recorded the highest share of global issuance ($215.7 billion annually) and a 5-year CAGR of 8.48%. Conversely, China recorded a 5Y CAGR of 8.45%, though its 10-year CAGR was -4.28%. Nevertheless, issues will arise after 2021, including regulatory and economic challenges. Japan experienced the largest changes, with a spectacular 324% growth in 2023 and a five-year CAGR of 11.54%, demonstrating market instability (Table 7.5).

In 2021, global equity issuance reached $1.05 trillion but dropped sharply by 61% in 2022. The US experienced a 77% decline, and the EU saw a 50% decrease. In contrast, debt issuance remained relatively stable; in 2023, total debt increased by 1.54%, whereas equities declined by 9.9%, indicating a potential shift toward debt financing. Nevertheless, equity markets remain highly sensitive to cyclical volatility, as the common stock CAGR over five and ten years stands at -5.21% and -4.40%, respectively.

In Japan and the European Union, capital issuance grew by 324% and 32.7%, respectively, while it decreased by 29.6% in China. These trends confirm that geopolitical risks and national policies are increasingly becoming important in shaping capital flows. Emerging markets (EM) have outperformed developed markets (DM) over the last five years, with a CAGR of 11.03% compared to 6.10%. However, in 2023, EM issuance dropped by 3.4% and by 18.8%, suggesting the impact of monetary policy tightening and regional crises affecting global capital flows.

The apparent 110.5% growth in the issuance of convertible bonds up to 2023 is interesting. It must be recalled, however, that these amounts are being discussed in terms of value rather than the number of issuances (fell by 69.8%). This rise contrasts with the short-term losses experienced in 2022 and indicates that investors are now more willing to adopt leveraged instruments amid high interest rates. Although total convertible bond issuance has remained relatively stable over the last decade, with a 10-year CAGR of 0.59%, volatility in the convertible bond market and the ongoing decline in issuance underscore the market's high sensitivity to monetary policy and macroeconomic shifts.

On the other hand, Table 7.6 clearly shows a high concentration in the global derivatives market. For example, North America accounted for 73.4% of the futures market and 81.1% of the options market (2023), with 10-year compound annual growth rates (CAGR) of 9.99% and 10.86% for financial futures and options, respectively. Europe accounts for 22.9% of equity futures (i.e., $2.12 trillion) and 17.2% of options (i.e., $385 billion). However, the European options market remains stagnant over the

**Table 7.6** Exchange-traded derivatives markets

| *Region* | *Futures (2023 level $B)* | *Futures 10Y CAGR* | *Options (2023 level $B)* | *Options 10Y CAGR* | *Market Share (Futures)* | *Market Share (Options)* | *GFC Impact (Futures) (2008–09 vs. 2006–2007)* | *GFC Impact (Options) :2008–09 vs. 2006–2007)* | *COVID Impact (Futures)* | *COVID Impact (Options)* |
|---|---|---|---|---|---|---|---|---|---|---|
| North America | $6,786.9 | 9.99% | $1,814.2 | 10.86% | 73.40% | 81.10% | -9.30% | -32.40% | -27.60% | -36.70% |
| Europe | $2,115.8 | 0.54% | $385.3 | -6.14% | 22.90% | 17.20% | -0.70% | 66.60% | -6.60% | -8.10% |
| Asia Pacific | $239.0 | -1.63% | $15.1 | 4.05% | 2.60% | 0.70% | -26.30% | -42.90% | -32.10% | -23.10% |
| Other Markets | $106.0 | 0.49% | $23.3 | 4.70% | 1.10% | 1.00% | 2.10% | 99.50% | -20.30% | -31.70% |
| **Global Total** | $9,247.7 | 6.34% | $2,236.9 | 4.83% | 100% | 100% | -7.00% | -3.40% | -23.00% | -32.50% |

Note: GFC (2008–09) and COVID-19 (2019–2020)
* "Futures impact/Options impact" (GFC 2008–09; COVID-19 2019–20).
Source: Author's elaboration on Bank for International Settlements (BIS) statistics (2023), exchange-traded derivatives statistics

long term (10-year CAGR of -6.14%), with structural problems and a loss of competitiveness relative to North America.

The CAGR of global futures over the last 10 years is 6.34%, with the market reaching $9.25 trillion in 2023. The growth of options, on the other hand, is at a 4.83% CAGR and is expected to reach $2.24 trillion in 2023. Nevertheless, the trend over the last five years has been downward: global futures declined by 23% (2020), while options fell by 32.5%. North American options recorded the largest decline of 36.7%, followed by Asia Pacific at 31.7%, Europe at 23.1%, and other markets at 8.1%. However, there was a robust recovery in 2023, and futures and options in the world surged by 14.9% (North America +15.1) and 23.9%, respectively (Table 7.6).

The Asia Pacific is the most paradoxical: the largest growth, yet the least market. The area has a CAGR of 4.05% for options, while futures contracted at -1.63% over the same period. With these numbers, Asia-Pacific accounts for only 2.6% of global futures trading and 0.7% of options trading. This implies that despite the rapid growth of Asian derivatives markets, they remain relatively shallow in terms of both total volume and liquidity compared with Western markets. In the meantime, other regions, such as Latin America, Africa, the Middle East, and Eastern Europe, have seen a 10-year CAGR of 0.49% in futures and 4.70% in options, with a global market share of approximately 1%. Understanding how systemic crises affect commodity markets shows large differences in sensitivity and strength across regions. The GFC had the greatest impact on commodity markets in Asia (-26.3%) and Central America (-9.3%). In contrast, during the GFC, European options surged by 66.6%, most likely because of increased hedging. Meanwhile, the COVID-19 pandemic had a major impact on both North America (-36.7% for options) and Asia (-32.1% for futures), with two major disasters occurring in each region.

Options markets in Europe saw a sharp 66.6% rise when the global financial crisis struck. This unprecedented performance is due to low trading volume in the run-up to the crisis and the use of options to hedge against risk in weathering such situations. The American options have risen by 32.4%, and the Asia-Pacific options have risen by a record 42.9%.

The COVID-19 pandemic affected every region to some degree, with negative effects. During COVID-19, North American options fell by 36.7%, other markets by 31.7%, Asia Pacific by 23.1%, and Europe by 8.1%. Futures markets were down sharply. For example, Asia-Pacific futures fell by 32.1% and North American futures by 27.6%, whereas European futures fell by a relatively small 6.6%.

Other markets (Africa, the Near East, and Latin America) were the only ones to record growth in GFC options (+99.5%). This unexpected growth shows that our markets rely less on global financial events and that domestic factors have a greater influence on prices and volumes.

During the first pandemic, global financial markets were protected by lower levels of integration. However, during the COVID-19 pandemic, these markets declined by 31.7%, highlighting stronger links among global financial markets.

## 7.4 The Shifting Landscape of Global Fixed Income

As the relationship between the US and China has become more complex over time, especially compared to the past century, current fixed-income markets bear witness to significant changes in the global economy. Over the past decade, the global fixed income market has grown significantly, as shown in Table 7.7, from $85.2 trillion in 2013 to $140.7 trillion by 2023. This represents a 65.1% increase, compared to a 73.7% increase in the equity market in the same period.

The ratio of fixed income to equity has risen modestly to 2.4:1 from 2.3:1. US dominance stands at 39.3% of the global fixed income market and 42.6% of the equity market in 2023, while emerging markets gain 4 percentage points in both asset classes.

Corporate debt has become the fastest-expanding component of the fixed-income market, rising by 107% over the last decade, and the gap between it and the dominant government bonds has narrowed considerably. Simultaneously, the financial sector maintained its 2023 ratios of 32% of the total fixed-income market and 28% of the equity market (Table 7.7).

Even though turnover in fixed income markets remains three times that of equity markets ($1.2 trillion vs. $0.4 trillion), liquidity in stocks grew by 100% (from 20% to 40%), while in fixed income markets it grew by 71% (from 70% to 120%). This signifies the growing maturity and equilibrium of international capital markets. Moreover, the ratio of bonds to equity in the Eurozone increased from 3.3:1 to 3.8:1, reflecting market depth. On the other hand, in the U.S., a 0.7:1 ratio indicates a greater reliance on equity financing (Table 7.7).

**Table 7.7** Comparative analysis: Global fixed income vs. equity markets (in trillions of USD)

| | *2013 Fixed Income* | *2023 Fixed Income* | *Growth (10 Y)* | *2013 Equity* | *2023 Equity* | *Growth (10 Y)* |
|---|---|---|---|---|---|---|
| Total outstanding | $85.2T | $140.7T | 65.10% | $66.2T | $115T | 73.70% |
| DM share | 86% | 82% | −4 p.p. | 79% | 75% | -4 p.p. |
| EM share | 14% | 18% | +4 p.p. | 21% | 25% | +4 p.p. |
| Sector breakdown | | | | | | |
| Government debt | $38.1T (53%) | $56.6T (44%) | +49%* | – | – | – |
| Corporate debt | $14.3T (20%) | $29.6T (23%) | +107%* | – | – | – |
| Financial sector | $24.2T (33%) | $41.2T (32%) | +70%* | $9T (28%) | $14.9T (28%) | *+66%* |
| Regional leaders | | | | | | |
| United States | $32.7T (38.4%) | $55.29T (39.3%) | 69.00% | $24.03T (36.3%) | $48.97T (42.6%) | 103.80% |
| Eurozone | $22.6T (26.6%) | $25.83T (18.4%) | 14.00% | $8.61T (13.0%) | $12.62T (11.0%) | 46.60% |
| Japan | $11.9T (14.0%) | $11.49T (8.2%) | −3.40% | $4.54T (6.9%) | $6.15T (5.3%) | 35.40% |
| China | $4.9T (5.8%) | $22.9T (16.3%) | 362% | $3.95T (6.0%) | $10.93 T (9.5%) | 177% |
| United Kingdom | $5.5T (6.5%) | $5.8T (4.2%) | 5.10% | $4.43T (6.7%) | $3.09T (2.7%) | -30.10% |
| Liquidity metrics | | | | | | |
| Average daily turnover | 70% | 120% | 71% | 20% | 40% | 100% |
| Turnover ratio | 1% | 1% | -0.1 p.p. | 1% | 1% | +0.2 p.p. |

Note: Data for China in this table refers to mainland China only, excluding Hong Kong SAR, to ensure consistency with WFE equity market data

Source: Author's calculation on data from the Bank for International Settlements (BIS) for fixed-income securities and the World Federation of Exchanges (WFE) for equity market capitalization, as presented in SIFMA Capital Markets Fact Book (2024)

During the period of low interest rates (2013–2021), the share of corporate debt in total fixed income rose from 20% to 23% as companies increasingly turned to borrowing in financial markets.

However, equities, due to their rising liquidity and growing role in emerging markets, are becoming an increasingly important capital-raising instrument.

Moreover, the US continued to dominate the global fixed-income markets, accounting for 39.3% of outstanding debt ($55.3 trillion in 2023) and recording annual long-term growth of 5.2% over the past five years, largely driven by robust issuance of Treasury and corporate bonds (Table 7.8).

However, the US market declined by 15% in 2022 due to rising interest rates, yet it still proved the dollar to be a safe-haven currency.

With a share of 18.4% ($25.8 trillion), the European Union is the second-largest market. However, growth has been modest, at just 1.3% over the past few years. The region is thus responding to the threat of market fragmentation. The fastest-growing major market is China, which now has the third-largest share at 16.3 percent ($22.9 trillion), up from 6% ($5.8 trillion) in 2013. In fact, it represents a phenomenal 16.5 % 10-year CAGR, driven by rapid domestic growth across the government and corporate sectors (Table 7.8).

The UK accounts for 4.2% of global fixed income, amounting to $5.8 trillion, with a 10-year compound annual growth rate (CAGR) of 0.5%. Although the market has been affected by Brexit uncertainty, it remains one of the most international and liquid bond markets in the world, particularly for foreign currency-denominated bonds. Canada has steadily increased its share, now holding 3.1% ($4.3 trillion), with a 10-year CAGR of 6.8%, driven by strong issuance from both the government and private sectors. The Canadian market benefits from close integration with US financial markets and a stable and well-regulated domestic investor base.

Australia accounts for 1.6% of the global fixed income market ($2.3 trillion). It has experienced modest growth, with a 1.3% CAGR, indicating a stable, mature market supported by a robust banking sector and a developed pension system. In contrast, Switzerland has a market share of 0.7% (US$921 billion) and is growing at 7.2%, largely due to its status as a hub for international capital. Singapore (0.5%, US$752 billion) leads Asia with a growth rate of 8.5%. Meanwhile, Hong Kong, although smaller (0.2%; $217 billion), continues to grow solidly at 7.0%, reaffirming its role as a key link to China and broader Asian capital markets.

**Table 7.8** Comparative analysis of global fixed income markets outstanding (2009–2023)

| | *Average Outstanding (2009–2023)* | *2023 Value ($ Billions)* | *Y/Y Δ (2023)* | *5Y CAGR (2018–2023)* | *10Y CAGR (2013–2023)* | *Crisis Impact* | *Share of Global (2023)* |
|---|---|---|---|---|---|---|---|
| United States | 38,548.00 | 55,298.80 | 6.00% | 6.40% | 5.40% | −15% (2022) | 39.30% |
| European Union | 21,488.90 | 25,829.70 | 9.30% | 5.50% | 1.30% | −12% (2022) | 18.40% |
| China | 11,050.60 | 22,913.50 | 5.80% | 9.20% | 16.50% | −18% (2011–12) | 16.30% |
| Japan | 12,668.60 | 11,495.70 | −4.60% | −2.1% | −0.35% | -8% (2015–16) | 8.20% |
| United Kingdom | 5,496.00 | 5,841.00 | 10.80% | −0.4% | 0.50% | −22% (2022) | 4.20% |
| Canada | 2,934.40 | 4,317.90 | 5.70% | 5.10% | 6.80% | – | 3.10% |
| Australia | 2,055.20 | 2,258.60 | −1.50% | 2.90% | 1.30% | – | 1.60% |
| Switzerland | – | 921.2 | – | – | 7.20% | – | 0.70% |
| Singapore | 411.9 | 751.9 | 14.50% | 8.80% | 8.50% | – | 0.50% |
| Hong Kong SAR | 135.3 | 217.1 | 12.20% | 7.00% | 7.00% | – | 0.20% |
| Developed Markets (other) | 1,955.20 | 3,794.60 | 1.10% | 2.90% | 15.70% | −22% (2022) | 2.70% |
| Emerging Markets (other) | 3,159.10 | 7,035.20 | 13.20% | 5.10% | 17.50% | −14% (2016) | 5.00% |
| **Global Total** | 100,449.90 | 140,675.20 | 5.90% | 5.20% | 5.10% | −12% (2022) | 100% |

Source: Author's calculation on Bank for International Settlements (BIS) data, via SIFMA Capital Markets Fact Book (2024), Table 1-09

Japan's fixed income market is projected to reach $11.5 trillion in 2023 (8.2% of the global total), accounting for 8% of total growth. The 10-year CAGR is low at -0.3% due to deflation and currency depreciation.

## 7.5 Conclusion

Overall, the multifaceted analysis concludes that there is a drastic reconfiguration of global capital markets. In fact, the Western triumvirate (US-EU-Japan) leadership has been particularly focused on fixed income and capital liquidity, while the Asia-Pacific region has led in key growth metrics. Regional paths are increasingly diverging. The Asia-Pacific region stands out as a major growth driver, with great depth, efficiency, and breadth, propelled by robust economic growth and supportive regional policies. In fact, the Asia-Pacific region achieved the best financial market results in market depth (158.3% of GDP), efficiency (148.3% of turnover in 2015), and breadth (3.43% compound annual growth rate among listed companies), with China leading. Europe is becoming more aligned and recovering more slowly, facing significant problems stemming from structural weaknesses and market fragmentation. On the other hand, the Americas remain an important global center but are increasingly vulnerable to international shocks.

Moreover, capital-raising methods have changed significantly. Corporate debt has become the dominant source of financing, with an average of 5,048 issues projected annually ($1,048 billion) and minimal to flat growth (CAGR of 0.27%). On the other hand, changes in monetary policy and shifts in the current cycle have significantly impacted the equity markets, with global issuance declining by 61% in 2022 and common stock posting a negative 10Y CAGR of -4.40%. Meanwhile, the rapid growth of convertible debt (up 110.5% by 2023) indicates that investors are seeking a combination of debt and options in a high-interest-rate environment.

In addition, the United States continues to hold significant shares of global options and futures markets, at over 81% and 73%, respectively. With a 10-year CAGR of 4.05%, the Asia-Pacific region exhibits the fastest growth in the options segment. However, its overall market share remains low, at just 0.7%. This shows that the region remains dependent on developed Western financial markets and risk-management systems.

## References

–Adekoya, O. B., & Oliyide, J. A. (2021). How COVID-19 drives connectedness among commodity and financial markets: Evidence from TVP-VAR and causality-in-quantiles techniques. Resources Policy, 70, 101898.

–Ali, M., Alam, N., & Rizvi, S. A. R. (2020). Coronavirus (COVID-19)—An epidemic or pandemic for financial markets. Journal of Behavioral and Experimental Finance, 27, 100341.

–Atri, H., Kouki, S., & Gallali, M. I. (2021). The impact of COVID-19 news, panic and media coverage on the oil and gold prices: An ARDL approach. *Resources Policy*, *72*, Article 102061. https://doi.org/10.1016/j.resourpol.2021.102061

–Bank for International Settlements. (2023a). Debt securities statistics: Global debt securities outstanding [Statistical data]. Available at: https://data.bis.org/topics/DSS

–Bank for International Settlements. (2023b). Exchange-traded derivatives statistics: Exchange-traded futures and options, by location of exchange (notional principal, in billions of US dollars). https://data.bis.org/topics/XTD_DER/tables-and-dashboards/BIS%2CXTD_D1%2C1.0

–Beck, T., Demirgüç-Kunt, A., & Levine, R. (2009). Financial institutions and markets across countries and over time: Data and analysis. The World Bank. https://doi.org/10.1596/1813-9450-4943

–Hassan, T. A., & Riveros Gavilanes, J. (2021). The global impact of the COVID-19 pandemic on financial markets. Review of Financial Studies, 34(11), 5136–5205. https://doi.org/10.1093/rfs/hhab046

–Li, W., Liao, Y., Albitar, K., & Li, Z. (2022). The impact of COVID-19 on stock market volatility: Evidence from GARCH models. Finance Research Letters, 45, 102140. https://doi.org/10.1016/j.frl.2021.102140

–Securities Industry and Financial Markets Association. (2024). *2024 capital markets fact book*. https://www.sifma.org/research/statistics/fact-book

–Securities Industry and Financial Markets Association. (2025). *2025 capital markets fact book*. https://www.sifma.org/wp-content/uploads/2024/07/2025-SIFMA-Capital-Markets-Factbook.pdf

–So, M. K. P., Chu, A. M. Y., & Chan, T. W. C. (2021). Impacts of the COVID-19 pandemic on financial market connectedness. Finance Research Letters, 38, 101864.

–Yousfi, M., Ben Zaied, Y., Ben Cheikh, N., Ben Lahouel, B., & Bouzgarrou, H. (2021). Effects of the COVID-19 pandemic on the US stock market and uncertainty: A comparative assessment between the first and second waves: technological Forecasting and Social Change, 167, 120710.

–World Bank. (2023). Global Financial Development Database [Dataset]. World Bank. https://datacatalog.worldbank.org/search/dataset/0038648/global-financial-development

–Zhao, L., Rasoulinezhad, E., Sarker, T., & Taghizadeh-Hesary, F. (2023). Effects of COVID-19 on Global Financial Markets: Evidence from Qualitative Research for Developed and Developing Economies. The European Journal of Development Research, 35(1), 148–166.

CHAPTER 8

# Conclusion: Crises as Catalysts of Structural Change

**Abstract** This chapter concludes the book with an analysis of three key transformations in the global economy. First, the shift to a multipolar structure in which the United States, Russia, and China collectively hold global income; second, the rise of debt as the main source of financing, especially after the dynamic increase in corporate debt; and third, the increase in the productivity of the financial sector, with a shift from bank lending to market-based financing. Regional differences in the resilience of financial systems are now apparent. While the Asia-Pacific region is very resilient, Europe faces structural problems, and North America maintains its lead despite growing instability. Overall, the crisis acts as a catalyst for change and highlights weaknesses in the global financial system.

**Keywords** Multipolar financial landscape • Regional financial resilience • Market financialization • US-China duopoly • Post-crisis transformation


M. Ganić, *Structural Change and Competitive Dynamics in Global Financial Markets*,
https://doi.org/10.1007/978-3-032-28906-3_8

## 8.1 Crises as Catalysts, Not Initiators of Change

The central idea of this book is that major financial crises, such as the GFC, the COVID-19 pandemic, and the 2022 Ukrainian crisis, do not create new financial hierarchies. Not to mention that they tend to become more widespread. Understanding current trends in the financial sector is crucial for policymaking. The book discusses the importance of macroprudential measures, particularly the obstacles faced by financial institutions that have previously relied on funding to support rapid credit growth. Furthermore, the crisis has shown that traditional balance sheets are not always sufficient to maintain financial stability. Fiscal or macroeconomic weaknesses can further weaken investor confidence. Six sections demonstrate the complexity of this conclusion.

The GFC identified weaknesses in the Western banking system. Excessive leverage, insufficient regulation, and rapid securitization contributed to the vulnerability of global financial markets. This led to a quick shift from traditional banking practices to market-based financing methods. Following COVID-19, digitalization, regional fragmentation, and the conflict between European stagnation and Asian disruption have become even more apparent.

Then, as the war in Ukraine unfolded, the geopolitical situation became unstable, and Moscow was removed from financial responsibility. New York, Singapore, Paris, and Amsterdam became key beneficiaries. In summary, crises often appear as the original structural changes, rather than serving as their causes.

## 8.2 Three Major Transformations in the Structure of Global Finance

The research presented in the book shows three key changes in global finance:

The global financial influence is moving away from Western dominance toward a more multipolar landscape. At the beginning of the century, the US, the EU, and Japan dominated global financial markets; however, the Asia-Pacific region, which was once aligned with both the US and China, is now gaining prominence. Chapter 2 highlights that the Asia-Pacific region's capacity exceeds that of other regions, reaching 158% of GDP and 166% of the stock market turnover ratio. Chapter 6 reports that China's corporate bond market has seen its beta coefficient decrease from 0.71 to

0.28, indicating less dependence on US economic cycles. Chapter 6 also indicates that the US-China duopoly now controls 55.6% of the global fixed income market, a sharp increase from 40.9% ten years ago.

*Expansion of debt markets is a key source of global capital raising*. Debt has become the dominant form of global capital raising. Chapter 6 shows a 107% increase in corporate debt and a 78% increase in fixed income since 2013. Chapter 5 shows that, after the crisis, bond issuance stabilized at 2.41% of GDP, or 0.85 percentage points higher than before the GFC. This cheap debt has become an important part of corporate finance.

*Market financialization and the weakening of the traditional banking model reflect* the shift from bank financing to capital markets. Chapter 1 shows the differences between the market-oriented American system (74.9% of the debt market) and the bank-centric European system (80.7%). Chapter 4 discusses how Basel regulations accelerated this shift by raising the cost of bank loans. Chapter 5 explores how the derivatives market, particularly FX swaps and forwards, has become the primary tool for currency trading. This reflects a broader focus on market-based risk management.

## 8.3 Resistance of Regional Financial Systems

A common theme of resilience runs through all chapters of the book, highlighting the diversity and adaptability of different financial systems. The Asia-Pacific region has the strongest resilience profile: the deepest market, at 158.81% of regional GDP, and a highly efficient equity market, with a turnover rate of 166.8. For example, market volatility rose significantly during the GFC and again during the COVID-19 pandemic. This resilience stems from the region's diverse sources of financing, including foreign direct investment, equity, and debt, as well as a cautious approach to external borrowing. In contrast, the Americas are experiencing greater uncertainty and exhibiting less resilience. The continued dominance of the USD (88.45% of currency turnover) and strong stock market performance, with the 10-year S&P 500 growth rate of 9.9% and the US market's 21.5% growth in 2023, suggests that the region's debt position deepened.

Europe exemplifies weak financial integration. After the GFC, Europe's market liquidity declined significantly. Meanwhile, the annual decline in the number of publicly traded firms and options remains at half of the 2008 level, indicating structural problems that are hard to fix, even if they are hidden. Africa, despite a modest annual growth rate of 6.04% in corporate debt, shows substantial volatility, with a coefficient of variation (CV) of 58%. The region has shifted from foreign direct investment (FDI) to debt financing, with the share of debt in external liabilities increasing from 26.46% to 32.67%.

# INDEX





M. Ganić, *Structural Change and Competitive Dynamics in Global Financial Markets*,
https://doi.org/10.1007/978-3-032-28906-3

GPSR Compliance

*The European Union's (EU) General Product Safety Regulation (GPSR) is a set of rules that requires consumer products to be safe and our obligations to ensure this.*

*If you have any concerns about our products, you can contact us on ProductSafety@springernature.com*

In case Publisher is established outside the EU, the EU authorized representative is:

Springer Nature Customer Service Center GmbH
Europaplatz 3
69115 Heidelberg, Germany

Batch number: 10852815

Printed by Printforce, the Netherlands